ATT

THEORY

OVERCOME ADDICTIONS USING COGNITIVE BEHAVIORAL THERAPHY . FIND RELIEF FROM DEPRESSION & ANXIETY WITH MINDFULNESS EXERCISES TO STIMULATE THE VAGUS NERVE AND YOUR EMOTIONAL INTELLIGENCE

WRITTEN BY **THERESA MILLER**

Congratulation on purchasing this Book and thank you for doing so.

Please enjoy!

No part of this publication may be reproduced, distributed, or transmitted in any form or by any means, including photocopying, recording, or any other electronic or mechanical methods, or by any information storage and retrieval system without the prior written permission of the publisher, except in the case of very brief quotations embodied in critical reviews and certain other noncommercial uses permitted by copyright law.

PRINTED IN USA

ANXIETY SERIES

"Certain of the interest shown on the topic, thanking my public for the daily follow up, I list those that are the current projects published, hoping to do something nice!"

Good reading...

ANXIETY in RELATIONSHIP expanded edition – Rewire Your Brain From Attachment Theory Of Anxious People. How To Break Bad Habits, Toxic Thoughts, Crucial Conversations, Worry And Return To Talk To Anyone

COUPLES THERAPY WORKBOOK – How to Reconnect With Your Partner Through Honest Communication. Overcome The Anxiety In Relationship And Build A Strong Emotional Intimacy Laying The Foundations For Unconditional Love

ANXIOUS in LOVE - How Stopping the Spiral of Toxic Thoughts and Anxiety in Relationship Overcoming Conflicts and Insecure of Couple. Abandonment and Separation is Never a Relief!

JEALOUSY in RELATIONSHIP – Manage Your Emotions By Overcoming The Fear Of An Insecure In Love. How To Sweep Away Anxiety With New Communication Skills, For A Healthy Couple

*"For better enjoyment, you CAN find all this titles also in audio format, on **Audible.**"*

MY FREE STEP-BY-STEP HELP

<u>I'll send you a free eBook</u>! Yes, you got it right. I'll send you my future projects, in preview, with nothing in return, just leave a realistic review on this eBook, believe me, it will be very helpful to other readers.

Thanks in advance!

Leave me your best email and my staff will send you a copy as soon as possible:

theresamillerauthor@gmail.com

TABLE OF CONTENT

INTRODUCTION

And you lived happily ever after...or at a minimum, you would if you were more interesting or attractive, or if you weren't so needy, or if you figure out what's wrong with you that makes your relationships work out badly. Maybe you've been with a partner for a long time, however, you struggle with the feeling that your companion keeps falling short and doesn't fill that hollow place in your heart.

You also suspect you are a part of the problem. They feel lonely and need companionship — not just a buddy to take a seat next to them at a movie, but a friend, a confidante, and lover to accompany them through the greatest of all adventures we call life. They regularly worry that their partner will bolt once they recognize "the real me." But sometimes they experience that their partners recognize the awesome things they do. But this isn't enough. After all, what if their performance falters?

Then there's the ever-present problem of whether or not they might really be there for them if they permit themselves to be vulnerable by trying to offer support, comfort, and reassurance. If you can relate to any of these struggles, then this ebook is for you. As a clinical psychologist, I have dealt with many people with diverse versions of these themes. Over the years, they have opened their hearts and lives to me, hoping for a tremendous alternative — and I consider that most of them realized it.

Therapy allowed them to discover the love they sought and pick companions who offered true love. With wiser choices, they created possibilities for increase and restoration. The result allowed them to revel in and nurture happier healthier relationships.

You, like a lot of my patients, may be armed with loads of information, expert advice, or a "tested formula" for success in relationships. It may come from your own family and friends, self-help books and articles, or even out of your therapist. You may have tried to fulfill the roles of Mr. or Ms. Right by socializing more or honing your online profile.

If you're already in a relationship, you may have practiced assertiveness and effective communicative skills, in addition to reminding yourself that you are worthy of love. Yet you still battle with feelings of loneliness or chronic fear of rejection.

There is a reason for this and there may be a solution. You started out studying relationships as an infant with your caretakers. I realize that's one of the clichés of psychology. However, it holds true. Your first training on how to nurture others, and on how cute you are, is based totally on the warmth, acceptance, and reassurance offered by your parents or others who took care of you. Though you cannot have been privy to this style till early life or adulthood (or perhaps it's unclear), your modern-day style might be fundamentally the same as what was nurtured in your childhood. If your early reports left you wondering about your sense of being worthy of love, scared of being rejected, or with an unquenchable thirst for reassurance, and you had poor nurturing in childhood, then you definitely experience it in this way.

It may also be the painful experiences later in life that lurked below the surface that intensified relationships. But the basic vulnerability to this attachment of partnered tension possibly developed in childhood. It's important to recognize that attachment-associated tension does not react to any obviously abusive or harmful parenting. In fact, the opposite is true. Many people with attachment-associated tension come from very loving homes. You may wonder why, then, might my attachment-related anxiety stay with me throughout my life?

To answer this, consider the endless variety of interactions you had together with your mother and father or other caretakers for the duration of your childhood, day after day, month after month, year after year. These interactions — though not all of equal weight — implicitly educate you in ways others will respond to you, teaching how worthy you are of being loved.

One critical lesson that I've discovered in doing this remedy is a little like gardening in that therapists provide people with what they want to grow. I listen, share my perceptions about their situations, offer compassion and guidance to teach them to nurture personal increase. In response, they (hopefully) discover ways to see themselves differently; reply to themselves in new, better ways; feel encouraged to chance alternatives (the unknown is always a touch scary), and learn to be different. But all of this has to show up at its own pace; it could be advocated, but it cannot be forced.

One crucial necessary detail is developing more self-cognizance. This consists of being aware of your thought, acknowledging and consciously experiencing your emotions, and knowing what makes you tick. These tasks can be tough, especially while you are facing unsightly or conflicting elements of yourself. However, they give you a higher appreciation for your struggles.

Such self-focus often allows human beings to feel an extra sense of well being and enables alterations — such as decreasing attachment-associated anxiety and the nurturing of healthier relationships. As vital as self-consciousness is, it's essential to recognize that it occurs in the context of courting yourself. And many people are too tough on themselves. Just as you'll attend to a harmed child by being nurturing, it's necessary to be compassionate towards yourself. Approaching your relationship struggles from this angle is what this ebook is about.

The explanations contained here are in an easy to understand language, and tells you how your relationship struggles were first formed, how this process made exchanges so difficult, and how these difficulties may be overcome so you can revel in a steady and lasting love.

While the main point of this ebook is to help you understand what you can do to find happiness in an intimate relationship, the ideas presented will also help you to recognize your ideal companion more easily. Sometimes, a window into your partner's world is exactly what you need to relate to his or her viewpoint, which in turn can help you nurture a healthier relationship.

The book is divided into four parts. The first helps you to understand your relationship struggles inside the context of attachment theory. Then, it opens the door to exchange through supporting you to identify limitations to nurturing your happy relationships. This explains how you can improve a steadier intimate relationship with a compassionate self-consciousness, which is basically being aware of your actions while also relating to them in an accepting and compassionate manner. "Lighting Up Your Love Life," offers suggestions for how — with a basis of compassionate self-cognizance — you can pick out a great partner and nurture a satisfied, healthful relationship.

CHAPTER 1

To see a beginning is to witness a miracle. This is where the story of every person's life of relationships and love begins. Infants need their caregivers for survival. So, thanks to Mother Nature, infants are hardwired with a want to connect to others, and the wherewithal to do it. For instance, they like to observe human being's faces, can get others to take care of them through crying, and are commonly comforted by way of being held or rocked.

All of this keeps their primary caregivers (normally their mothers, and secondarily their fathers) interested in defending and nurturing them. As children become mobile, their continued need for assistance to exist motivates them to live near their mothers. A toddler who ventures out will appear back at Mommy's side for reassurance.

It's in those early years, starting with infancy, that people first learn the way relationships can help them experience safety. Anyone who's spent time with infants and young children understands these behaviors. Ainsworth's studies help display that through innumerable interactions with their mother and father — subtle or now not so diffused — children's manner of bonding seeps into their very being.

This style of bonding will become a working model that sets their expectations for the way others will respond to them, as well as for the way they experience themselves. Sometime later, researchers confirmed that the attachment process changed into romantic love (Hazan and Shaver, 1987; Feeney, 2008). While nature affords the attachment system as a way to ensure the child's survival, attachment bonds developed inside that person and were felt as love — in both early life and adulthood. Children are searching for the love in their Mom and Dad as if their lives relied upon it (which they do). It's no marvel that youngsters who generally tend to get disappointed easily have problems being soothed by their mother and father. They also have a tendency to struggle with being dissatisfied with problems as adults and are unable to discover a consistent, dependable sense of soothing and safety in their romantic relationships.

Primitives and Ambassadors

The components of the human mind that concentrate on survival are around for a prolonged time — actually, since the sunrise of our species. I call to those warring components our "primitives." Do not forget your primitives as your beasts within. The primitives operate without your permission. They're first in the chain of command as survival reflexes and perform to trump all your different wishes and desires. They may be sellers of war (fighting and walking away) and defeat (surrendering and playing dead). Fortunately for us, we have a more evolved, social part of our brain. We can legitimately say it's wired for love. Unlike the primitives, the ambassadors interact in a refined, civilized manner. You'll take into account your ambassadors as your diplomats inside.

Actually, a number of our primitives feature as ambassadors sometimes, and some of our ambassadors have primitive functions as well. For our purposes in knowledge of couple's behavior, it's useful to oversimplify a bit and recall them as opposing camps. Let's look closely.

The Primitives

Our primitives are geared to wage war. Whether it's a hint of conflict or enormous warfare, they're capable of defending us. They allow us to experience, and react, and to be the primary receivers of data, both internally and externally, from the body. This makes them fast at identifying risks and threats, and expedient while managing those risks and threats.

In reality, our primitives have all the benefits a few years of evolution can afford, like integration, efficiency, and speed. They were first to arrive on the scene and likely will be the remaining ones standing at the top (death). And importantly, how are you capable of perceiving them in motion in your dating?

Your Primitives in Action

In essence, the primitives function consists of a series of commands, nearly like that employed by the military. When danger or risk is perceived, a sequence of events unfolds that leads both to warfare and to the primitives going on alert. All this takes place inside our brains and bodies, very speedy, at a level normally beyond our focus. Yet if we study carefully, we can hit upon the evidence. And once we've accomplished that, we can believe how we'd have an impact on the method. To make the sequence easier to locate, I've defined three critical stages: Red alert! Ready the troops! Action!

STAGE 1: RED ALERT! The number one line of defense for the primitives is to perceive a chance to sound the alarm, loud and clear: "Watch out! Danger is here!" This is often administered through our most primitive system, the amygdalate, almond-shaped system inside the brain. The amygdala usually sweeps the environment for signs of hazard and does so for the duration in a down-and-grimy fashion. In other phases, they indiscriminately grab evidence they find. They don't have an awful lot of a technique, nor do they stop to analyze whether or not the danger is real or imminent. They scream alert, and assume one among the ambassadors will make a careful evaluation and step in to correct any errors or inaccurate assumptions made through the primitives in an instant.

Intelligence ought to be analyzed earlier than getting into conflict. However, evaluation takes time, and time may be trouble when danger is afoot. The amygdala, in large part, runs the show between them once they experience threat by one another's facial expressions, vocal inflection, sharp movements, or harmful phrases. Instead of two complete brains at war, it's a case of dueling amygdala — sort of like the Wild West gunfighters honing their twitch before reaching for their pistols. Like Darius and She, companions are on constant lookout for threatening symptoms and signals. Specifically, the proper-facet amygdala alternatives alert for dangerous facial expressions, voices, sounds, movements, and postures. The left-facet amygdale alert for dangerous words and phrases.

Consider Franklin and Leila. After courting for a year, Leila is frustrated by Franklin's hesitancy to ask for her hand in marriage. She is set to leave and date others. While having dinner one evening a week after Valentine's Day, they get into a fight. After a prolonged duration of listening to music, Leila, at the passenger side, all at once shuts off the stereo.

"Can we talk?" she asks, looking ahead.

Franklin's body stiffens as he utters, "Sure."

His amygdala has picked up the tone in her voice and, therefore, the events that just occurred: the silence, the turning off of music, and the question, "Can we talk?" His amygdala has grabbed onto all this and is no longer available to Franklin's complete consciousness, and his frame prepares for something vaguely warlike.

Moments earlier, Leila had been contentedly listening to a song with the phrase, "Goin' to the chapel…." The image captured her amygdala, and she suddenly felt disturbed, almost before she knew what happened, her amygdala had sounded an alarm, the subsequent primitive within the chain of command jumped to interest: the hypothalamus.

The hypothalamus is the primary primitive liable for getting our minds and our bodies prepared for movement; it directs the pituitary and adrenal glands to launch chemical substances vital for action. These glands are messengers and foot soldiers below the direct command of the hypothalamus. Together, these primitives shape the majority of our strain reaction system, freeing substances — inclusive of the acute-pressure reaction hormones adrenaline and cortical — into our bloodstream.

The speedy-appearing adrenaline amps us up and gets us ready for fight or flight, while the slower-appearing cortical allows us to adapt to stress with the aid of reducing infection and harm in our frame. The continual balancing act between these chemicals feeds messages again to the hypothalamus: ought we keep combating or is it time to withdraw the troops?

As soon as the alarm for war has been sounded, the hypothalamus offers us three options: we can fight, flight, or momentarily freeze while we decide whether to fight or flight. One way or the other, the decision is made: "Ready the troops!" Just because the amygdalate sent out an alarm without thinking about the accuracy of statistics, the hypothalamus responds to the amygdalate without questions. Again, the assumption is made that the ambassadors will come along later and smooth everything out, as wished.

With Whom Do You Connect When You Are Sincerely Dissatisfied?

At times, your attachment has grown; like turning on an internal homing device for which the goal or partner is an attachment determinant. When an adult's emotion works well, he has a stable style of attachment. But human beings with an insecure sample of attachment don't fully or continuously find such consolation in their partners or in others, an indication that their "homing tool" is malfunctioning.

Current research (Bartholomew and Horowitz, 1991) indicates that attachment patterns (whether or not steady or insecure) are fundamentally based on underlying "working models" (or default ways of relating) — an operating version of self and a running model of others. The running version of self is your sense of worth or unworthiness of being loved.

As you can imagine, when you feel unworthy of love, you also fear being rejected and struggle with attachment-related anxiety. You might understand this as tension — a feeling of anxiety or nervousness. But you could also experience it as a different feeling of distress, such as sadness, loneliness, or anger. Adults and children with a constant experience of unworthiness live as though their attachment device, or homing tool for an attachment determinant, is stuck in the fully "on" function. If you become aware of this, you'll be constantly searching for reassurance from an attachment parent and have a chronic sense of feeling alone, rejected, or worry about being rejected. Even at the less intense tiers of attachment associated anxiety, humans can feel somewhat inadequate and worry about being unable to emotionally manage rejection.

People have a running model of others — an expectation of whether or not others can be emotionally available to them. To the quantity that they anticipate others won't be there for them, they get an uncomfortable sense of being close to others and tend to avoid it. This is what psychologists call attachment-associated avoidance.

Some individuals are so sure that others won't be emotionally available that they decide to be fully self-reliant. They do everything to try to keep themselves from feeling they want to rely on someone else. It's as though their attachment gadget or homing device is stuck on the "off" function.

Exercise:

How Much Anxiety and Avoidance Do You Feel in Your Relationships?

To find out how much attachment-related tension and attachment-related avoidance you wallow in, rate yourself on a scale of 0 – 10, with 0 being no way and 10 being that you completely relate. Hold onto those numbers so that you can use them later for assessing your attachment style.

Other people don't want to be as near as I would like to be, and my choice to be so close regularly scares them away. Whenever I have a partner, I ask myself and am concerned that I'm no longer as desirable as him/her or other people. I'm constantly concerned that he/she doesn't care about me as much as I care about him/her. I'm particularly worried that he'll/she'll find someone else when we are not together.

Rating Attachment Related Avoidance — I am an independent person, so I don't want to be devoted in dating. It makes me uncomfortable while my partner desires to depend upon me or to talk a lot about his thoughts and emotions. When I have problems, I generally tend to keep them to myself and figure them out on my own, and I'd like it if my partner would do the same.

Rating: Nine

Three Styles of Attachment

As I've defined, attachment patterns can be understood by combining how people relate to themselves (which could create anxiety) and to others (that may result in avoidance). By dividing the dimensions of tension and avoidance as excessive and low, the following four possible combinations are created: preoccupied: high anxiety, low avoidance; fearful: high anxiety, high avoidance; dismissing: low anxiety, high avoidance; secure: low anxiety, low avoidance.

The original research on the attachment concept labeled the attachment styles as being categorically extraordinary from each other — just as a girl and a fish are categorically exceptional unless you are given to believing in mermaids. However, contemporary research studies (Griffin and Bartholomew, 1994) suggest that this isn't true. Instead, unique attachment styles represent "blurry" groups that display tendencies, however, they no longer have to be taken literally. Combining levels of avoidance and anxiety works a lot like blending primary colors. Red and yellow make orange. However, adding only a little yellow to purple creates an orangey-crimson; and adding only a little red to yellow creates an orangey-yellow. A similar dynamic takes place with two dimensions of attachment.

Consider Ann, who is high in tension and very low in avoidance, and Dan, who is also excessive in tension, but only a little low in avoidance. Keep in mind Heather. She had always felt insufficient as a person and exhibited a preoccupied attachment style. Her husband, Alan, reinforced this feeling with his frequent cognizance of her mistakes and shortcomings. He finally divorced her, leaving her to struggle with an even greater experience of being unlovable. But with therapy, she ceased severely wondering about this negative view of herself. She became capable of recognizing that Alan was overly critical. Then she met Sam, who valued her thoughtfulness and creativity. She basked in his love and warmth, which melted her self-rejection and helped her to feel more comfortable with being valued by someone else.

Romantic relationships frequently serve as a special possibility to revise your attachment style to become healthier — an opportunity that this book permits you to recognize. Consider the styles of your past companions, or maybe your friends and colleagues. Your attachment-related tension can activate you to make quick, and often inaccurate, emotional judgments of others. As a result, you might misunderstand your partner's emotions, struggles, and behaviors. This can cause big problems in dating. By now you know your lover's attachment style better and can understand him. Also, with the aid of having a close hold of secure attachment, you may understand the blessings of operating toward this for yourself. You could recognize how having a securely attached partner will let you.

One last vital caveat before you study the attachment patterns: a simple look at these styles will leave you with the impression that the handiest "right" manner to pursue healthful dating is to have a stable attachment style. This impression would be wrong, but the "excellent" way to connect is to have a romantic relationship that makes you happy. If you tend toward having a preoccupied style of attachment and are married to a person who has that tendency, yet the two of you are happy — then accept this and enjoy it.

Your fashion and life condition are proper for you. As it happens, one giant way (but no longer the best manner) of finding happiness in your relationship when you are unhappy is to move toward a stable fashion. But as you examine your life and what you may need to alter, it is crucial to keep your eye on the actual "prize": happiness in love.

Just as they are cushy with their relationships in general, securely attached people are also happy with their sex lives. Placing a high priority on emotional intimacy, they tend to remain faithful, feel comfortable discussing intercourse, and experience the pleasures that it has to offer. If you're anxiously attached and fortunate enough to have a securely attached partner, you will find this a stable and positive opportunity that allows you to increase a more secure attachment style.

Preoccupied Attachment: Desperate for Love. Meet Rachel — a person you would possibly relate to. Her boyfriend is affectionate and shows interest in her, but she doesn't understand what to think because it doesn't fit together with her self-perceptions. She's sure that once he understands "the real me", he'll leave her. So she continuously worries that he won't get along with her on the weekends. And whenever he doesn't respond at once to her texts, she assumes he's heading away from her. This looming opportunity for rejection is overwhelming, and she is preoccupied with that fear.

People like Rachel who have a preoccupied attachment style are touchy to the possibility of being unnoticed or rejected by their lover, whom they need to guard them. They use hyper activating strategies to keep their attachment machine "turned on" (or activated), which ensures they will be sought after for a dependable attachment type.

For instance, they often overreact to troubles and underestimate their ability to cope; they may constantly reexamine troubles in the past, present, and future. In creating all of those negative emotions and thoughts, they heighten their need for an attachment type and are essentially crying out for one.

Unfortunately, the ones who try this can also feel chronically overwhelmed, vulnerable, and needy. Their sensitivity to any viable signs of rejection by accident instigates fights and creates distance from their intimate relationships. It's a given that sooner or later their companions will misunderstand them, be physically unavailable, or no longer respond in a caring enough manner; but humans with preoccupied attachment styles will view this with alarm.

A clear instance of this is how disenchanted Rachel becomes when Phil immediately respond to her texts. Although people with a preoccupied style might begin a relationship and feel intoxicated, they're then apt to see their companions as unloving (or not always available), untrustworthy, and in all likelihood, unfaithful.

This leads them to be possessive. To make matters worse, they're regularly unable to calm down enough to forgive their partners for any wrongdoing, so their relationships are unstable and easily disrupted via troubles. Because of their attachment needs and struggles, they feel unsturdy.

Some people with a preoccupied attachment style prepare their lives around trying to show that they're worthy of love or trying to distract themselves from their bad emotions. This interferes with their potential to show themselves authentically or to pursue personal interests.

Rachel, for instance, did so during college, however, she settled for a job as a receptionist after graduation — and remained in it for years — because she couldn't decide what to do with her bachelor's degree in English. She became concerned with her image and what others thought of her performance. It didn't go well for Rachel. Humans with a preoccupied style regularly deliver their troubles and sadness with partners into reality.

Also, the constant strain and tension they sense often causes health issues. Just as they do with the rest of their lives, people with a preoccupied attachment type base their sex lives on a need for reassurance and avoidance of rejection. So even though they revel in being held and caressed without sincerely looking for more sexual intimacy, they turn to sex to get the reassurance of attractiveness that they seek.

Men try to sense, cherish, and find acceptance through a girl. They tend to be greater at being sexually reserved and to look for their companion to be sexually responsive and pleased. By contrast, women try to experience, cherish, and find acceptance through a man. They tend to be much less reserved, or on occasion promiscuous. Companions or situations manipulate their intercourse lives, and they are often uncomfortable speaking with their partners about sex.

Think whether you relate to him at all or whether or not he sounds like anyone you know. He is happy with his independence, his self-sufficiency, and his commitment to his sales activity. He enjoyed spending time along with his ex-girlfriend, Chris, however, wasn't too upset when she ended their relationship. To him, she made a big deal of his commercial enterprise trips by asking him to call her, although she only requested an occasional check-in. He felt she wanted to talk about her emotions and their courting "all the time."

Although he sometimes feels neglected when his buddies speak about their girlfriends, he says he's not bothered by it and prefers to spend the time alone. What Andy denies, even to himself, is that he actively minimizes and avoids his emotions. This feature of people with a brushing off attachment style, puts them at risk of tension and depression. People with a preoccupied style and those with a dismissing fashion are also susceptible to consider that their partners will no longer reliably be there to guide or console them. But they protect themselves by unconsciously using deactivating techniques to "turn off" (or deactivate) their attachment device, keeping them from being in the untenable position of feeling a pull to rely upon an undependable partner.

They effectively suppress, keep away from, or forget about their emotions and attachment desires. For example, at the same time as Andy often seemed kind as he helped Chris with her finances, which she appreciated, it allowed him to remain in a distant and superior role, which elevated her terrible emotions about herself. At other times, Andy might keep a distance and reply to Chris's tries to be emotionally intimate by telling her that she was "too needy." This, of course, extended her self-doubts.

Generally unaware of their emotions, disregarding people are not geared to cope with the emotionally frightening experiences. For instance, whilst their partners irritate them, they try to decrease or deny their anger. However, that anger remains beneath the surface, frequently making them aggravated and unforgiving. This dynamic does not bode well for their relationships.

This dynamic is most problematic for anxiously connected partners, who generally tend to interpret the disregarding accomplice's anger as proof that there is something wrong with them. So why doesn't the disregarding companion simply leave? Even those with a dismissing style need comfort and connection. Dismissing people couch their sexualities inside the same remote and self-protective way as they interact in relationships in general. Because physical or sexual touch can weaken their defenses, many are uncomfortable with connecting via touch, which includes hugs or gentle caressing. They may remain emotionally remote by proscribing sex to one-night stands or short-time period relationships.

When they are in intimate relationships, they tend to no longer be affectionate and can be emotionally disengaged during intercourse. This can leave anxious partners feeling unattractive and unworthy of love.

Fearful Attachment: He has been this way since he was a kid. By the age of fourteen, he'd basically been looking after himself because his father was angry and his mother became busy looking after the family collectively whilst operating long hours. He thinks of himself as flawed, needy, helpless, and unworthy of love. He believes that others know something is wrong with him and holds their distance. Although he would like a committed, romantic, relationship, he avoids getting close out of fear that he'll be rejected or misunderstood.

This struggle between an extreme worry of rejection and a desperate need for reassurance and closeness is usual of human beings with a frightened attachment style. When they're no longer heading toward relationships, they emerge as behaving in contradictory and confusing ways. However, when they understand their companions as getting near, they experience the risk of getting hurt, so they instinctively appear to shield themselves from their partners, turning to deactivating techniques to avoid intimacy.

In Ahmed's case, he could spend his weekends repairing old furniture, permitting the time he could be together with his girlfriend (when he had one). This consistent tension of being too near or remote leaves fearfully attached people chronically distressed, insecure, extraordinarily passive, and emotionally distant. Not surprisingly, they have an excessive chance of anxiety, depression, and different emotional struggles.

Convinced that their partners are emotionally unavailable, fearfully connected people tend to view their companions in a particularly terrible light and have difficulty empathizing with them. For instance, when Ahmed was courting Amanda, a fearful stype stewed in their emotions as opposed to directly dealing with them. Probably due to their experience that they're unworthy of love, the fearfully connected person tends to stay in their relationships even when the relationships are severely troubled or even abusive. On the opposite hand, because of their discomfort with intimacy and being appreciated (though it's what they desperately want), they are likely to experience something is wrong and quit a relationship, even if they're in love and their companion is without a doubt caring.

Sometimes this means using casual intercourse as a safe way of coming together emotionally while seeking to meet their want for comfort, acceptance, and reassurance. They might do that with one-night stands or short-term relationships that end when they begin feeling vulnerable. When they're less centered on meeting their attachment desires and are within the mode of protecting themselves, they're likely to avoid sexual intimacy and its accompanying vulnerability.

If you haven't already done so, review the four attachments and decide which one you most resemble. For instance, are you essentially secure with a tendency towards doubting your self-worth (being preoccupied)? Another way you could check your style of attachment is to measure your scores on the dimensions of hysteria and avoidance. Get a clean sheet of paper. Draw a horizontal line and label it "Anxiety". Place evenly spaced tic marks along it, numbering them from 0 to 10 (from left to right). At the five, draw a vertical line and label it "Avoidance". Again, make tic marks alongside it and range them from 0 to 10.

Where Do You Fall in Your Relationships? Using your two rankings, plot where you fall in the quadrants and place a dot there. You will notice the category quadrant that you fall into, however, you'll also see how near you are to each of the alternative quadrants. The less extreme you are on every size, the less your traits will match the prototypical style of the quadrant you are in. Along with revealing your attachment style, it shows which category you fall in on an attachment-associated anxiety and attachment-associated avoidance.

Once you've identified your personal attachment style, you need to take a look at the attachment style of your companion or past companions. You can rate them the same way you rated yourself. Limit the usage of your observations and their behaviors. You can also have contemporary companions rate themselves if they are open to it; the gain of this is that it could open some illuminating and intimacy-constructing conversations.

In each case, their style of attachment will help assist you to become better at finding the desired partner data.

How can we move toward and away from (both actually and figuratively) the ones whom we depend on? It constantly amazes me that couples may be together for fifteen, twenty, or even thirty years, and still not understand each other. In a lot of ways, they don't realize what makes each other tick.

Not everyone responds the same way in courting. We come to the table oriented towards a certain style. We may understand our partner's style, however, it is may not be on a conscious degree. Unhappy partners often claim lack of expertise: "If I knew you were like this, I'd in no way have married you" and claim ignorance, "I just don't understand what planet you're on", throughout the connection.

Growing up, our mother's and father's or caregiver's styles of affection set the standard to which we adapt. Simply positioned, as we will notice in the next chapter, our social wiring is set at an early age. I gift ten key ideas that display the ways to avoid commonplace pitfalls that deter or undermine several relationships. These principles are:

- creating some bubble permits companions to keep one another secure and steady.

- Partners can avoid the struggle with sex when the security-seeking elements of the brain are positioned comfortably.

- Partners relate to at least each other in the main as

  - anchors (securely connected),

  - islands (insecurely avoidant), or

  - waves (insecurely ambivalent).

- Partners who are experts on every other ability delight and soothe each other.

- Partners with busy lives ought to create and use bedtime and morning rituals, as well as reunion rituals, to remain connected.

- Partners must characterize the first go-to human beings for each other.

- Partners must save each other from being the 3rd wheel when concerning outsiders.

- Partners who need to stay collectively must study to fight nicely.

These standards are supported by the most modern technology, but permit me to remind you: you don't need to comprehend the technicalities of the science to understand these concepts. I have accomplished that for you. I've easy and enjoyable to understand. I promise not to roll in the medical jargon. As I said, life is complex enough already.

Each exercise includes activities to help you follow the precept discussed therein. You may do many of them on your own, but if you can, do them with your partner. There may be a specific irony here. A vital premise of this ebook is that happy couples share closeness and togetherness, yet most people tend to study books — even books with relationships — alone. So I encourage you not to follow this trend. Share what is in the course of this ebook with your partner. You will get more out of it.

For instance, I generally pay attention to new mothers and fathers as they say, "I will by no means do what my mom and dad did to me," and yet, despite their most ardent wishes to no longer to repeat their mother's and father's errors, during times of misery, they will do precisely that. I don't say this with judgment; it's a failure of human nature and biology.

Most partners audition for relationships blind to who they are and how they are stressed to narrate in a devoted couple universe. As in all try-outs, they undertake to put themselves forward within the most pleasant light. It wouldn't make a good experience for someone on the first date to say, "I spent lots of time alone as a child and I still do. I don't like me by myself to be intruded upon. I'll come to you when I'm equipped. And don't bother coming to me, because I'll think you're annoying me, and I don't like that." An equally quick way to send a date walking for the hills would be to say, "I tend to be clingy and to get irritated once I feel abandoned. I hate silences and being ignored. I by no means appear to get enough from humans, yet I don't take compliments properly because I don't believe people are being sincere, so I'm apt to reject something nice."

No one likes to be classified, yet we tend to categorize human beings around us because we've got brains that, through nature, organize, sort, and compare records. In truth, people have been defining the human circumstance for centuries, and they continue to doing so today. We are liberals or conservatives, geeks or Goths, atheists or religious fanatics, Scorpios or Capricorns, either from Mars or from Venus. As long as we don't use these classes to debase or dehumanize everybody, they can assist in helping us understand each other.

A key premise of this ebook is that partners can take advantage of having an owner's guide for each other in a relationship. A crucial function of this manual is that it lets you define, describe, and label your partner's predilections and relationship style. If you can recognize and understand each other's patterns, it's less difficult to resolve issues as they arise. Having the feeling that "I recognize who you are" makes it less complicated to forgive and to be really supportive.

The styles I gift right here are neither new nor my very own. They are drawn from research findings, first made famous by Ahmed Bowlby (1969) and Mary Ainsworth and her colleagues (Ainsworth, Bell, and Stayton 1971) almost half of a century ago, explaining how infants shape attachments.

Over the years, I have determined that maximum partners fall into one of three predominant relationship patterns. I offer those patterns to you with a couple of caveats. First, in case you discover you couldn't determine which style fits your partner or yourself, don't try to push it. I have supplied the patterns in their pure shape. In reality, the "mileage you get" though the statistics may vary. Although the sizable majority of people do fit with one or another of those three patterns, not everyone does. In fact, many people may be a blend of various patterns, which from time to time makes it tough to pick out the most salient one. If that is the case for you, no worries. You can hold both in mind and use whichever suits you best in a given situation.

Second, my motive in describing these styles is to inspire, recognize, and know-how for what are every day human traits. Please do not take them as individual defects. Definitely don't flip them into ammunition against your companion. Rather, see these patterns as representing the necessary adaptations every person makes in becoming an adult.

How We Develop Our Style of Relating

As I've stated our social wiring is set at an early age. Whether we grow up feeling stable or insecure is determined with the aid of how our parents or caregivers related to us and the world. If they tended to spend more face-to-face time with their child; be more curious and interested in their child's thoughts; be more focused, attentive, and attuned to their child's wishes; and be more influenced to errors or accidents, in order repair the goodness of the connection, they devised a stable environment for the child. The dynamics of this early relationship leave their mark at a physiological degree. Neuroscientists have determined that youngsters who receive masses of fine attention from adults tend to increase more neural networks than youngsters disadvantaged of social interplay with grown-up brains. The attachment and anxiety of steady kids tend to be properly integrated, and so these youngsters are capable of dealing with their emotions and impulses.

Their amygdalate isn't overcharged and their hypothalamus conducts ordinary operations and remarks communication with the pituitary and adrenal glands, the opposite cogs inside the risk and stress wheel, turning that gadget on and off when appropriate. Because of the right relationships early in life, stable kids tend to have a properly developed brain so they're adept at reading faces, voices, emotions, and bodies. In particular, their orbit frontal cortex is nicely developed, with neural connections that offer comments to their other ambassadors and their primitives. Compared with insecure youngsters, they generally tend to have more empathy, better ethical judgment, greater control over impulses, and greater regular control of frustration.

In general, steady children are more resilient to the slings and arrows of social-emotional strain and do better in social situations. Steady dating is characterized by playfulness, interplay, flexibility, and sensitivity. Good feelings predominate due to the fact that any bad feelings are speedily soothed. It's a terrific vicinity to be around! It's a place where we can anticipate laughter, pleasure, relief, comfort, and shelter. When we experience this type of steady basis as a child, we send it forth into adulthood. We end up as what I'm calling an anchor.

However, not everybody had relationships in their early youth that felt stable. Perhaps we had numerous rotating caregivers, without one who changed into being available or dependable. Or perhaps we had one or more caregivers who often valued something other than courting, which includes self-preservation, beauty, youth, performance, intelligence, talent, money, or reputation. Maybe one or another caregiver emphasized loyalty, privacy, independence, and self-sufficiency over dating fidelity.

Almost anything can supplant the fee of dating, and frequently when this occurs, it isn't by choice. A caregiver's intellectual or physical illness, unresolved trauma or loss, immaturity, and so on can intervene with a child's experience of security. If this takes place, then as adults we come to relationships with an underlying insecurity. That can lead us to hold onto ourselves and avoid an excessive amount of contact, alternatively viewing ourselves as an island in the ocean of humanity.

The Three or Four Things That Make Your Partner Feel Bad

In reality, we all have a handful of issues with the particular power to make us sense something is amiss. These problems usually originate at some point in adolescence, and we take them into our adult relationships. For instance, you may have been picked on as a child, and so you maintain a vulnerability whenever a person tries to tease you. It affects you to this day. Or as a child, you were told you were ugly or stupid, and now you continue to sense you are less attractive or intelligent than others. Perhaps

44

someone from your early life always had to be proper and continually made you seem wrong.

Here's another scenario. Let's say that in your adolescence you experienced an outstanding deal of chaos and disorganization from your mother and father. The loss of order currently upsets you, and you are also bothered by folks that are careless, messy, and disorderly.

The second area of study is attachment theory, which explains our biological connection or bond with others, starting with our earliest relationships. In a nutshell, some people are stable in their relationships, whilst others are insecure. Insecurity can lead us to stay remote from a partner or to harbor ambivalence about relating. However, insecurity manifests, as we will see in Chapter 3, its insidious consequences on a relationship if we don't try to rewire the dysfunctional inclinations begun early in life.

In the meantime, to realize the intention of pairing up with any other person, we will trust what takes place as an infant. The infant feels loved and stable, therefore, the person enjoys the feeling of being loved and being cared for. We call this number one attachment dating because the child and caregiver are bonded, or attached, as a minimum to each other. You may say that is regularly an "infant bubble" — it's just like the couple bubble occurring at some point of infancy. If at an early age we experienced protection and love we may want to trust, we carry this with us. As adults, we're ready to shape new number one attachment relationships.

On the other hand, if at an early age our relationships with caregivers have not been steady, and consequently the caregiver didn't appear to care about being with us over all other matters, we are probably going to be apprehensive about being involved in relationships. (We will communicate in additional depth about attachment in the next chapter).

We will change what came when we were babies. However, if the early influences are affecting how we sense relationships, if they hinder our capability to forms of bonds we would like in our lives now, we need to resolve them.

For a few couples, a remedy is necessary for this kind of rewiring. Other couples are already equipped to talk about and reimagine their issues with minimal external input.

Let's take a look at what it takes to make a bubble for your companion who keeps everything secure.

Making the Pact

The couple bubble is an agreement to put your relationship first. Therefore, you tell each other, "We come first." During this, you cement your relationship. It's like making a commitment or taking a vow, or like reinforcing a vow you already took with each other.

Sometimes human beings say, "I don't need to commit until I am sure this problem with you won't be a drag." I've heard variations of this from both men and women in my years as a couple's therapist. There's no better way to daunt a likely companion than to imply that he or she is inadequate for you or to insist that they prove himself or herself earlier so safety is assured. This kind of technique is doomed to fail. Partners stepping into a bubble agreement want to invest and completely respect it. They need to be together this way.

When companions don't honor the couple bubble and bitch that they aren't being nicely cared for, usually the rationale is that they get precisely what they paid for. "Buy a part of something, and you get part of something." My answer is that if she or he is so far from okay, then he or she shouldn't be a contender. However, this isn't the case. I see companions who've cautiously and thoughtfully chosen every difference but worry about the problems that come up after trying to understand each other better will become deal breakers. Typically, those troubles contain the wonderful characteristics everyone chose in the other person, which they now realize also contain worrying elements.

For instance, you adore his sense of humor, however you now dislike that he cracks jokes once you need him to be serious. In another case, you can appreciate her musical talent, however, be annoyed when she wants to practice the piano in place of strolling with you. Sometimes companions at some stage in this situation need to bargain: "Can I simply take you with the parts I want, and we'll toss the rest?"

Sorry. This isn't a burger joint, where you get to hold the pickles and lettuce. You have to buy it as it is. I understand this could sound harsh. But I have said this to couples. They typically respond by way of retaking stock of things. They recognize the toll their ambivalence is taking on the relationship. Then they are ready to move on in one direction or the other.

Are We Ready for Commitment?

I'm not suggesting you try to make a bubble prematurely. It's crucial to consider that the informal relationship and courtship levels are exclusive from a relationship that's shifting towards, or has turn out to be imbued with permanence. Within the starting of a relationship, we are besotted and captivated through the completely happy hopefulness and mutual admiration we sense. Our brains wash in dopamine and adrenaline, two chemical substances that greatly enhance pleasure and focus.

As soon as we leave the other's orbit, our brains struggle with dwindled serotonin, a chemical that continually calms tension and obsession. We find ourselves thinking, "When will I see him again?" or "Should I call her tomorrow?" and other thoughts that send us to the billions of fishes within the social sea. Of course, this shared love fest obscures the very truth that we don't yet know each other well. In the moment, who cares?

We are kind of a rocket that is released with sufficient acceleration to get it to the edge of space, however, we might need to jettison its booster and engage a greater accelerant to travel farther. During a brand new courting, we're just excited to be aiming for the stars and anticipate we'll determine the entirety as soon as we get there. But if we would like the connection to face an opportunity of accomplishing its destination that is precisely what we've got to determine if we can reach. Holding the couple bubble is also to burden one another with the duties of devotion and being concerned for the other's protection, safety, and proper being. This mutual burden determines the degree of shared gratitude and valuation you each can enjoy. When the going gets tough, the couple bubble is all you'll hold onto while you're courting together. This doesn't imply you won't make mistakes or accidentally get hurt. It doesn't imply you will in no way make a choice that does not put yourself before the connection, nor that you shouldn't. These things will happen, irrespective.

However, it does mean you may keep each other for your fundamental statement: "We come first." Then, if either one of you makes an error, the other will offer a mild reminder: "Hey, we agreed to try to do differently." The transgressing companion can say, "Oh yeah, my bad," and speedily fix matters.

Exercise: The bubble trouble meter. After you and your accomplice have entered into a bubble settlement, the next step is to observe it. Although an agreement has been made, maintaining the bubble can be a process. It's ongoing. You may say the bubble assumes a life of its own. And intrinsically, you must periodically take its pulse. During this exercise, you may develop a bubble trouble meter. By that, I mean you'll become aware of the signs that tell you that your couple's bubble isn't always imparting the safety it has been designed to supply.

1. Over subsequent weeks, study the extent of closeness you're feeling between yourself and your partner. Of course, closeness will naturally undergo a degree of ebb and flow. What you want to avoid is getting ebb so severe as to warrant sounding an alarm.

2. Pay special attention to those moments of trouble. What is taking place? What are you feeling, and what is your partner feeling? What sorts of things do you tell each other? For instance, you'll probably say that you want to explode and leave your partner alone at such times. This then can be a sign for your meter.

3. Make an inventory of the precise symptoms you become aware of. Share those with your companion. Discuss how you will recreate your bubble, and enhance it to forestall any further annoying incidents.

Remember: the bubble protects you both! It's yours, so keep it smooth and polished for another day. The first guiding principle of this book is that creating a few bubbles allows partners to stay with one another and remain secure. Together, you and your partner can create and retain your bubble.

You made an agreement, now you need to work it out. What is it your partner most wants from your relationship (e.g., sex, money, commitment)? You're in this together. It works only if both partners stay committed to the course rather than saying, "You stepped over the line first."

Here are a few assisting principles to help you:

1. Devote yourself to your companion's sense of protection and safety and not your estimate of what it should be. What can feel secure and stable to you, may not be what your partner feels *from* you. Your job is to recognize what influences your companion and the way to shape his or her sense of security.

2. Don't pop the bubble. Because the couple bubble has its foundation as an essential, implicit, and absolute feeling of safety and security, neither of you should have to worry that the bubble is going to pop. Acting in an ambivalent manner, or taking a stance, is not part of the connection, and undermines the protection you've created. If this is allowed to persist, one of you may be forced into an

untenable position and may lose all the benefits of the bubble you have so carefully constructed.

3. Confirm the bubble is collectively maintained and honored. Note: this is frequently co-dependency. Co-dependent companions get over everything differently, while ignoring their very own desires, which results in resentment and other emotional distress. In contrast, while partners form a new bubble, each agrees on the principles accordingly. For instance, I can say my partner must be available to me on the occasions I demand, however, I want to make myself available too, without watching for her or him to move first. Then, if my lover doesn't fit our agreed-upon ideas, we've got some fixing to do. If both partners maintain our concepts, neither one of us is going to be upset.

4. Decide to apply your couple bubble. It gives a steady location for you and your companion to ask one another for help. It's your primary way of assisting and protecting each other. For instance, every time you and your companion input social conditions, especially ones involving tough people, you will ensure you'll both be protected through your bubble. As Greta and Bram did, work together so you'll figuratively hold fingers through the event. By holding hands, I mean remaining in contact with each

other, tracking each other, and being near at a moment's note. Eye contact, bodily contact, whispering, hand alerts, smoke alerts — whatever! Decide together in advance how you'll address difficult people. Perhaps you will hold fingers or sit down next to one another in their presence. In the meantime, recall that splitting up to deal with tough people or situations leaves you vulnerable. Together, you will be formidable.

Strengths of the Three Varieties of Touching

Three varieties of relating when speaking to me: psychologists use phrases like securely attached, insecurely avoidant, and insecurely ambivalent. To make it a little lighter, the alternative terms of anchor, island, and wave suffice.

Clearly, there are advantages to being an anchor. Given the selection, most older people could choose to feel steady or not. But we all carry something specific to the table. Imagine what an uneventful place this world would be if it had been the other manner. To maintain this focus, I'd start summarizing the strengths of each type.

As you study the three couples for the duration of this chapter and analyze more about the three patterns, see which type displays the connection for yourself and your accomplice.

The Anchor: "Two are better than one." Mary and Pierce were together for twenty-five years. They raised two kids, both of who are now out of the house. Lately, Mary and Pierce spend longer times dealing with their aging mother and father than with issues pertaining to their offspring. When Pierce's widowed mom was diagnosed with Alzheimer's disease, the couple observed themselves fighting the numerous options. Both have rewarding but demanding careers in the criminal field. They may have to bring Pierce's mom into their home for care. Their conversations lead to seeking out a medical facility for Pierce's mother. It went something like this.

"I want you to tell me exactly how you feel," Mary says, looking carefully at Pierce with a purpose to not omit any subtle conversation written on his face.

"Of course, you know I constantly do," says Pierce. "Honestly, because we had that long talk the other night, I have to mention I'm feeling a degree of relief."

"Because we discussed transferring your mother out of her home?"

"Right." He pauses, searching deeply into Mary's eyes, not hiding the pain hovering underneath his relief. "I suppose it's taken a load off me to recognize that staying here might not be the best lifestyle for her."

"You realize, I used to be worried you'd be upset with me once I stated what I thought would be the best choice," Mary says quickly. "I wasn't positive we were on the same page. My mother and father are still healthy, so this isn't the same for me."

Pierce smiles. "Yes, I admit I was quite disappointed at first. But I thought about it. I know you have been trying to figure out what would be best for everyone — you, me, and my mother."

"Exactly," says Mary. "If it were my mother, I'd want the same from you. This isn't about getting my way. It's about us, collectively. If you accept this as true, we must find a way to help your mother here, or, at the least, I'll work with you on that. I may disagree. But I won't fight you."

"Thanks," says Pierce. "And thank you for not overreacting after I started to get uptight."

"Honey, I had a pretty good feeling of what's going on for you," Mary says gently, then pauses with a twinkle in her eye. "You realize, after these years, I have the manual on you."

Pierce smiles back. "You certainly do, and I'm so glad — even though it's a heck of a long manual, with all my quirks and foibles."

Mary offers a chuckle. "You realize I wouldn't have you ever any other way. Besides, the manual you have on me isn't exactly the abridged version."

Pierce pauses and sighs deeply. "When I consider it rationally, it's clear that it wouldn't do to bring Mom here."

"Honey, if we put our heads together, we will find a way to make a first-rate decision. Arranging our schedules so we can each visit her is feasible…" Mary stops because she sees Pierce nodding his head and his eyes tear up.

"And deliver her right here for meals as often as we can," he says, picking up where Mary left off. She wipes a teardrop off his cheek, and he grabs her hand and kisses it. "Actually, I suppose I'll feel better as soon as I see my mother nicely sorted in a great environment."

"I know you will," says Mary. "Whatever comes up, we'll cope with it. As we usually do, yeah?"

"Yup. You recognize," Pierce adds, hugging her, "I so appreciate being able to talk with you about all this."

They each got here to the connection feeling secure in themselves as individuals. Of course, anchors don't always pick to be with other anchors. An anchor can mate with an island or a wave. In many cases, these matches result in the opposite partner becoming more of an anchor. Let me say this again because it's crucial: anchors can pull no anchors by turning into anchors themselves. Of course, the reverse can occur. An island or wave can pull an anchor into turning more insecure.

As anchors, Mary and Pierce are capable of offering safety to one another, skills they learned from early caregivers who placed a high value on dating and interaction. Their Mom and Dad were attuned, responsive, and sensitive to their signals of distress, bids for comfort, and efforts to communicate. Both Mary and Pierce have recollections of being held, hugged, kissed, and rocked as children. They remember seeing a loving gleam in their Mom's and Dad's eyes. Neither Mary nor Pierce feels the opposite is overly needy or clingy. And neither feels anxious about getting too close or moving too far away.

When they need to be apart for some reason, they make frequent contact by cell phone and e-mail, greeting each other with liveliness and suitable cheer. Together or apart, they are unafraid of any bad consequences, as changed into the case while Mary recognized what she thought might be of high quality for Pierce's mother.

They respect every other's emotions and treat one another as the first source of news and bad information. Each takes a cautious observation of the alternative in private and public, minding cues that signal misery and responding quickly to offer relief. In a lot of these approaches, they construct a mutual appreciation for their couple bubble and regard themselves as stewards in their mutual experience of safety and protection. Each has attempted to understand how the other works and to use this knowledge on a daily, if no longer a moment-to-moment, basis.

This couple views themselves to be in each other's care and understand that the lifeline they keep, their tether to each other, is what offers them the strength and courage to face each days' stresses and demanding situations of the world. Because their dating is stable, they can continually flip to it and use it as their anchoring tool amidst life's outer chaos.

Anchors aren't ideal human beings; however, they're generally satisfied people. They have feelings of gratefulness for the things and people in their lives. People tend to be attracted to anchors because of their strength of character, love of humans, and complexity. They can make selections and bear the consequences. Anchors take precise care of themselves and their relationships. They don't easily give up on a relationship if the going goes rough, or when they become frustrated. They are unafraid to admit errors and are quick to mend injuries or misunderstandings as they stand up. In those approaches, they're proper at coping with a relationship's demanding situations that might weigh down non-anchors.

Exercise: Are You an Anchor?

"I get along with a wide variety of people."

"I love people, and they tend to like me."

"My close relationships aren't fragile."

"Lots of touching and affection is great with me."

"I'm equally comfortable when I'm with my companion and when I'm alone."

"Interruptions from my cherished ones don't upset me."

Now let's examine a couple who function in a totally different way.

The Island:

"I Want You in the House, Just Not in My Room…Unless I Ask You."

Chianti and Carlos, each a specialists in their early forties, early in their marriage now not to have youngsters and alternatively embellish their courting with masses of tours and adventure. Chianti held off on getting married because she felt her profession as a journalist didn't permit her time to dedicate herself to another character. But then she met Carlos, and he treated her like a kindred spirit.

After their wedding, they built a home that covered separate areas: his and hers. Carlos had his track room, with a small bed for nights when he wanted to stay up late. Chianti designed an office where she sought to write and watch television without being disturbed. Their master suite turned into a wired excessively fast-paced Internet so each could use it on respective sides of their oversized king bed.

Problems rose rapidly after their wedding. Chianti's interest in sex began to wane. Carlos became accustomed to taking turns starting up sex, however, Chianti stopped making moves and began rejecting his advances. The intense eye touch they'd so frequently enjoyed for the duration of courtship become replaced through television shows, movies, and conversations from across the room.

Exercise: Are You an Island?

Do you see yourself or your partner from our discussion at this point? Here are some statements which might be common to an island. See if any ring a bell for you — either for yourself or your partner.

"I know how to take care of myself better than anyone else possibly can."

"I'm a do-it-myself sort of man or woman."

"I thrive when I can spend time in my sanctuary."

"If you upset me, I have to be by myself to calm down."

"I often feel my partner wants or wishes something from me that I can't give."

"I'm most comfortable when no one else is around."

"I'm low maintenance, and I prefer a partner who is also low maintenance as well."

Exercise: Are You a Wave?

Do you think you or your accomplice are a wave? Here are a few common statements; see if they apply to you or your accomplice.

"I take better care of others than I do of myself."

"I frequently feel as though I'm giving and giving, and never getting anything back."

"I thrive on speaking to and interacting with others."

"If you disappointed me, I have to talk it out we can patch things up."

For the most part, this is a superb assumption. However, as I mentioned earlier, despite their suitable features and benevolent intentions, ambassadors can be pretty obnoxious at times. It's proper: the ambassadors can pass wild, or wimpy, or just weird in everyone, no exceptions. Anchors generally tend to have the maximum balanced ambassadors. On the rare occasion that a number of their ambassadors pass wild, anchors possess different ambassadors which can corral the wayward ones quite fast.

Islands and waves, on the other hand, often grapple with greater severe ambassador disparities. During times of misery, islands and waves have one element in common: each has an ineffectual orbit frontal cortex.

The orbit frontal cortex, remember, is the ruler of ambassadors and primitives alike. It's our orbit frontal cortex that determines whether or not we move to battle. For this reason, islands and waves are at higher risk of getting into conflict if their ambassadors get wild or otherwise fail to toe the line. The wild islands tend to have heightened primitives and wild ambassadors. This is a result of having problems connecting on a non-verbal stage.

Of course, this imbalance is natural for an island and normally might lead to lawsuits in settings aside from romantic relationships. In an all-out conflict, an island's left brain gets hijacked by primitives and can end up threatening you by using attack or retreat tactics. To avoid this, ideally, you can use verbal friendliness. Provided your very own left brain does not go wild, talk your partner down. Be reassuring, calming, and rational. Try: "I understand what you're saying and it makes sense" or

"You're right about that" or "You make an awesome point."

A wild island frequently has little experience of what he or she is feeling and is bad at speaking of feelings or understanding the emotions of his or her partner. The lover of an island may additionally have problems doing this, irrespective of whether or not that individual is an island too.

The Wild Wave

If your companion is a wave; he or she may also insist on an excessive amount of verbal assurances of love and security. This is the reverse of what we see with an island, which is much less vulnerable. With a right mind long past wild, your partner can also seem overly preoccupied with the need for assurances and seem overly expressive, dramatic, emotional, tangential, irrational, and irritated. Under strain, a wave may be unforgiving, punishing, rejecting, and inflexible.

During a conflict, a wave will generally focus attention on the beyond and stay away from the present and future. In an all-out war, the wave's right brain gets hijacked through the primitive and can become threatened by pursuing a resolution through connecting. In this situation, the connector makes use of the physical and emotional connection as weapons. Again, it seems like an ambassador, but it acts like a primitive.

To avoid the explosiveness of two right brains at war, avoid lashing out non-verbally on your partner. If your right mind has not gone wild, disarm your companion with non-verbal friendliness. Touch her or him gently; offer a peaceful presence. When you do speak, be reassuring and soothing.

Third Guiding Principle

The third principle of this ebook is that partners relate to each other as anchors, islands, or waves. You and your companion need to emerge as familiar with each others' courting styles. We get to recognize our partners so we can be equipped as managers of our partners in a satisfactory manner.

By ready managers, I suggest companions who are specialists of one another and recognize the way to move, shift, motivate, influence, soothe, and inspire one another. In contrast, companions who are not professionals to one another tend to create a mutual feeling of danger and insecurity. They don't enjoy couple bubbles. These partners additionally tend to want the alternative to change, listen to them, or do matters the way they do, and ultimately agree that they coupled with the wrong man or woman. Sadly, these partners merely recreate the insensitivity, injustice, and insecurity of their youth, never in reality understanding what is within their best interest.

For many humans, closeness brings both the promise of protection and security. This increases the question, how do you get what you need and want from dating, while avoiding what you worry might happen? This quandary is much like stealing honey without being stung by a bee. The diplomacy by which we have to work to get the honey, by avoiding getting stung, in intimate relationships is the degree to which we feel fundamentally insecure.

But here's the rub: if we feel insecure in close relationships, there's no way to end up more stable without being in one. In other words, as far as relationships go, we are hurt by human beings and yet we may be healed most effectively by being with others. And that's correct. It is totally viable to be an anchor by spending time in a close, dependent, secure relationship with another person. That person can be a therapist, or it may be a primary romantic companion who's an anchor or close to becoming one.

Though the purpose of this ebook isn't mainly to transform you or your partner into anchors, its ideas will guide you in the direction of a greater steady courting. Spend sufficient time in a secure relationship, and you'll turn out to be an anchor.

There are some helpful ideas for you:

1.Discover your partner. Using the examples presented in this chapter, find out what you don't yet know about your accomplice. What first-class courting style describes your partner? And at the same time, what style pleasantly describes you? As I noted before, please resist the temptation to apply this typology as ammunition towards one another. Like any effective tool, it can inflict damage if used improperly, so use it with compassion in your courting.

2.Be unapologetically you. Our project in dedicated relationships is not to change or become a different person. Quite the contrary: our venture is to be unapologetically ourselves. Home is not an area to feel chronically ashamed or to pretend we're a person we're not now. Rather, we can be ourselves at the same time as retaining our sense of obligation to others and ourselves. And as simply as we are unapologetically ourselves, we should encourage our accomplice to be unapologetically him or herself. In this way, we offer each different unconditional recognition. Of course, being unapologetically ourselves doesn't imply we are reckless or uncaring about how we treat others, or that we can use this as an excuse to be our worst selves. For example, if your accomplice is untrue or in any other case hurtful to you, he or she can't say, "Tough. This is who I am." No. This is a time where an apology is in order. In fact, whenever your partner voices hurt, you want to focus much less on being unapologetically yourself and more on tending to your partner's needs and concerns. Remember the primary guiding principle: creating a couple bubble allows partners to keep each other safe and steady. Your mandate is to be unapologetically yourself as long as you additionally keep your partner safe.

3.Don't try to trade your accomplice. You could say that we all trade, and additionally that we in no way change. Both are true. And this is why recognition is so important. We can and do change our attitudes, our behaviors, or even our brains over time. However, the fundamental wiring that takes place during our earliest experiences remains with us from cradle to grave. Of course, we can trade this wiring in out of the ordinary ways via corrective relationships. Sometimes these changes remodel all but the final remnants of our remembered fears and injuries. But this should no longer be the aim of a couple's courting. No one modification from essentially insecure to fundamentally secure under situations of fear, duress, disapproval, or danger of abandonment. I assure you that will no longer happen. Only via attractiveness, excessive regard, respect, devotion, support, and safety will everyone gradually grow more secure.

CHAPTER 2

The protection of younger children depends on caregivers being close and attentive. Even as youngsters mature into adolescence and younger adulthood, they still rely on their mother and father, though the discern-baby relationship adjusts significantly. They develop their network of attachment and may also rely upon other family members, mentors, clergy, or close friends. And then, significantly, they often look to a romantic partner (subsequently a spouse) as their foremost attachment to help them experience safety and to assist in their pursuits. However, the "closeness" method is something of a unique piece for a person other than a young child.

Adults are powerful in using mental representations, or images, of attachment for an experience of comfort. Considering your partner, figure or close pal can provide you with the sense that they may be emotionally close, permits you to symbolically go back to them as a secure haven and a stable base. Over time, you might come to identify so much with positive caregivers that you include their way of relating to you into yourself, enabling you to keep an experience that you value and you generally expect that others will be supportive. Unfortunately, the more you struggle with attachment-related anxiety, the much less in all likelihood you will genuinely believe that others will provide for you.

As a result, you will have greater problems using intellectual representations as a secure haven to self-soothe or as a steady base for exploration. (I will return to the idea of intellectual representations later within the book because developing them is essential to lessen your tension and misery in relationships.)

Preoccupied: Grasping for Closeness — Some children understand their Mom and Dad as inconsistent. It can be due to the fact the parents are unavoidably focused on pressing life situations or on their very own emotional needs. The baby's inherent sensitivity is also a factor. Whatever the reason, children who question whether or not their parents are available are extraordinarily disillusioned by their Mom and Dad not being there for them.

This is a function of a preoccupied attachment type. Driven with the aid of their attachment desires, such children do anything they could to get their Mom's and Dad's attention — and as adults — to get their companion's attention.

Ahmed Bowlby (1961) mentions, the originator of attachment theory, referred to them as a hyper activating strategy. Demanding people become "hyper activate" in their attachment devices as their cries for attention end up more strident, making them more dissatisfied and regular cause battles in their relationships. For instance, they could demand their partner assist them in various ways, try and keep regular contact, or grow to be too difficult and possessive.

People with preoccupied attachment desire focus intensely on keeping others near, on the price of their own pursuits, and from time to time even their own values. This leaves them empty, without an experience of themselves that they can be precise about. Instead, they depend on someone else, -- a parent, friend, or spouse -- for approval and what pursuits to pursue and a way to respond to various circumstances. They are often encouraged with the aid of an outside image or goals (including economic wealth) as a manner to obtain approval.

Unfortunately, this search for outside approval keeps them from performing, which makes them feel as though they are forever seeking but missing approval just as they did with an attachment parent. Thus, they're left without the feeling of the closeness they crave and without a fantastic sense of themselves and are incapable of pursuing their very own pursuits.

Dismissing: Making It on Your Own

While some children are preoccupied with looking to get and preserve their Mom's and Dad's attention, others cease seeking to connect. As Bowlby (1961) explained, after a child's protest was repeatedly unanswered, or was answered too harshly, the child sees despair. Then, whilst he eventually gives up all hope of being reassured and protected, he detaches — attempting to deactivate his attachment gadget by shutting down his emotions and his need for a caregiver — and ends up being extraordinarily self-reliant. As a person, he's not going to experience the closeness that includes romantic relationships.

This characterizes the dismissing style of attachment. If your partner tends to a dismissing fashion, you might sense that he distances himself, instead of softening, in reaction to your reaching out in a supportive manner.

The purpose of this reaction is that he will not risk being let down later; so he retreats and ends up being even more distant. Similarly, when you are disappointed with your partner, he probably appears emotionally disengaged and unbothered. In all likelihood, however, he fears being rejected.

Dismissive human beings lose out on all fronts. Unable to behave on their preference for connection, they may be neither sincerely independent nor capable of feeling near an accomplice.

Fearful: Lost in Relationships

Some children grow up with parents who have their own strong attachment issues: they experience their Mom's and Dad's as sometimes emotionally available, every so often scared, and sometimes even horrifying. This variation is difficult and frightening. Those children are unable to discover a manner to continuously meet their attachment wishes. They don't discover solace in both deactivating (trying to go it by myself) and hyper activating (acting out for attention and acceptance), so they try to use both sorts of strategies in a disorganized manner. This creates a chaotic and puzzling sample in relationships called the fearful style of attachment.

In adulthood, their intimate relationships are often stuffed with struggle and puzzling dynamics as they pursue both closeness and distance. Not surprisingly, they're not capable of achieving a snug and comforting experience of closeness or a healthful feel of autonomy.

Exercise: How Well Do You Balance Autonomy and Closeness?

Relationships are, of course, more like an ongoing, dynamic balancing act than achieving some continuously held equilibrium. With that in mind, which of the following shows satisfactory representations of your ideal relationship? And which picture best represents your current relationship or your most recent one? These styles are expressed inside the following statements:

Secure Style:

- I am cushy and share intimate thoughts and emotions with my companion.

- I revel in pursuing hobbies other than my partner.

- I sense love through my companion even if we pursue pastimes separate from each other.

- Even when we disagree, I believe that my partner will still appreciate and understand me.

- I am comfortable in relying on my partner and having my partner rely upon me.

Anxious Style:

- I am most comfortable while my partner and I proportion all of our thoughts, emotions, and pastimes — when we appear to have merged into one.

- I am inclined to pursue what my partner enjoys, putting aside my own pastimes.

- I am willing to defer my values and evaluations to my lover's values and evaluations.

- Whenever I sense my baby being distant, I make moves to reconnect (for instance, often calling or texting); or I act angrily, including retreating or being nasty.

Avoidant Style:

- I am uncomfortable in sharing intimate mind and feelings with my companion.

- I take pride in being self-reliant enough to not need my partner.

- I am uncomfortable depending on my partner.

- I am uncomfortable with my companion depending on me.

- I enjoy pursuing interests apart from my companion.

In doing this exercise, you might need to draw overlapping circles and write your own descriptive sentences that better depict your dating. (We people are complicated, so it's okay if your description includes conflicting sentences). Now bear in mind how properly your relationship meets your desires for a:

Safe Haven: During stressful times, how are you able to rely upon your partner to offer you a sense of consolation, protection, and assistance?

Secure Base: How does your partner help you pursue your goals apart from your courting? How nicely does your relationship help you feel good about your sense of who you are?

During infancy, children are almost swimming in feelings. Their interactions with their mother and father are strongly guided by using their basic purpose of survival and their accompanying need to feel secure. A part of their mind called the amygdala is sensitive to threats to their protection. It is quick to react to possible risks, which include hunger, being on its own, or falling. It reacts reflexively, without evaluating risks and adjusting its response primarily based on the actual threat.

When you are strolling through the woods and feel a rush of worry at the sight of a stick which you mistake for a snake, you can thank your amygdala. Modulating this response is the characteristic of the hippocampus, but that part of the mind doesn't begin to function till children are between two and three years of age. Until then, all dangers are perceived similarly and trigger a determined look for a safe attachment figure to guard and soothe them.

This feeling is what neuroscientist Jack Panksepp refers to as primal panic (referenced in Ahmedson, 2008); and it continues to be precipitated into adulthood whenever humans feel threatened. It also regularly kicks in once they worry about dropping their partner or other primary attachment determinants. Depending on your attachment style, you will feel primal panic stronger or much less frequently; and you will be more or less effective in managing it. The same is true of your partner if you have one. The result of these extraordinary reviews has a massive effect on your dating.

In the next three sections, I talk about how the aggravating, avoidant, and secure attachment styles affect human being's emotional stories and the way they control the other's stories.

Emotions? What Emotions?

Children with a more avoidant style of attachment block their emotional reactions to threats. They are inclusive of their primal panic about the unavailability of caretakers. With time, they keep their attachment machine deactivated, and they no longer try to connect with their mother and father or battle with separation. Later in their lives, they're disconnected from their partners. It's essential to understand the tendency to distance oneself from feelings. Stress hormones surge while oxytocin ("cuddle hormone") tiers remain low. So, even though ignoring, suppressing, or denying feelings can frequently help to handle minor stressors, this technique is severely flawed.

When human beings with avoidant attachment styles can no longer forget about their feelings because their pressure or courting issues have emerged as so excessive and chronic, they often don't realize how to manage their feelings. This puts them at risk for the usage of unhealthy approaches to coping. Their emotions are also leaking out despite their reputedly calm demeanor. For instance, an avoidant man might calmly speak about his girlfriend being "this sort of bitch," and even denying any anger, unaware that his chest is tight and his heart rate is up.

You should take into account whether this commonplace dynamic is what's going on when you assume you're calm, however, it is uncharacteristic while saying or doing hurtful things. (If your partner tends to be the avoidant one, this dynamic may explain why you are disillusioned at times whilst your partner seems to be calmly speaking about serious problems.)

The Chemistry of "Secure and Happy"

Some children are fortunate enough to have a Mom and Dad who continuously nurture and calm them after they are upset. The more this happens, the better they turn to their parents — and the greater they produce the hormone oxytocin, which offers them a degree of feeling of protection and connection. When children (and adults) are upset, oxytocin brings down their range of strain hormones, adrenaline, and cortical. Over time, these responses help them to become comfortable with their full range of feelings and combine them into their lives. They end up as securely attached adults who are capable of handling their emotions, addressing private troubles, and efficiently handling conflicts.

It may be heartening to research that, as an anxiously attached individual, you may "earn" secure attachment — together with all of its blessings. You can also reduce your attachment associated anxiety and other distress by choosing a securely connected companion.

Exercise: Understanding Yourself in Context

The more clearly you recognize how your hyper activating or deactivating techniques develop, the more appreciation you will have for why you do what you do now. As you complete this exercise, be patient with yourself. Deepening your self-knowledge in this area can be nurtured, but it cannot be forced to appear all at once, so you may want to revisit this from time to time.

Make note of when you operate hyper-activating or deactivating techniques. Return to your responses from the previous exercise, "Can You Relate to 'Anxious and Overwhelmed'?" Think about them — maybe even talk with someone you accept as honest and discuss this with them. Make sure you have a very good understanding of your use of hyper-activating techniques. If you frequently use deactivating techniques to maintain a distance, you may have trouble doing this because you're possibly out of touch with your feelings. In that case, I suggest you look for comments from friends you trust and who think nicely of you. Ask them what you do to distance other people. Consider whether you used those same, or similar techniques as an infant. If you did, then reflect on what may have triggered you to do that. Sometimes you may gain insight by considering another baby in that identical situation.

Example: Jane's final two boyfriends told her, "You are simply too needy." Although she complained that neither of them were very affectionate men, she knew they were right. She worried constantly being afraid that they were about to end the relationship, so she would incessantly call and text them, looking for reassurance that they still cared. When she took into consideration this dynamic, she realized that it reminded her of how she felt when her father died. From then on, she was afraid of being too close to anyone because she feared they would leave her.

Again, don't count on a deeper self-cognizance to appear overnight. Journal, make notes and talk with reliable people appropriate for this exercise. But deliver it in a relaxing way; then go back to it again after you've had a chance to be open to new insights and perspectives.

With time, greater information of your styles will let you control your emotions, both within yourself and in your relationships. To nurture a healthier way of connecting in romantic relationships, remember how your relationship might be better if you do not have an extra-strong secure attachment. As you consider this, it's essential to be able to know how you no longer want to be the terms of secure attachment to help you discover happiness. But if something works for you, it will need to be in the direction of a steady attachment associated tension and attachment-related avoidance dimension.

Fortunately, as I've mentioned, you can increase this greater secure style as an adult. This system is what psychologists call "earned safety." There are two basic pathways, and they intertwine. First, you appear to the outside world. You need to begin by growing a courtship with at least one emotional attachment. If not a partner, then you can start with someone else, which includes a circle of relatives, pals, clergypersons, or a therapist. It could even be God.

Remember, attachment is the ones you sense you could turn to in times of misery and who are supportive of your attempts to enlarge your private horizons. The more you enjoy feeling frequent and protected, the more you will believe that you are worthy of affection and that others can be loved and comforted by you — giving you some "earned safety."

The second technique to developing "earned security" is to directly nurture a part of yourself that makes you aware of your reactions and to reply to those stories in a greater and more compassionate manner. I will provide an explanation in section 5 how together, as compassionate self-attention, those two processes will let you divulge your heart's content to reassurance and acceptance by using others, to experience their help even when you are by yourself (as intellectual representations of attachment), and to essentially be an attachment parent to yourself.

The path to healthier relationships includes you with others. Teaching you a way to achieve this is what the exercises of this ebook are for. To start, I'll assist you to make sure you perpetuate your cutting-edge attachment style in ordinary life, and what's averted you from selecting a healthier course.

The Three or Four Things That Make Your Partner Feel Good

How many people recognize the way to spontaneously make their companion sense satisfaction and feel cherished? I'm speaking of a phrase, a deed or an expression geared toward one's companion meant mainly to uplift him or her.

I have seen clients married for thirty years who appear dumbfounded while challenged to brighten, flow, charm, or otherwise enamor each other. Yet this capacity to spontaneously and predictably shift or raise your partner's mood or emotional nation is an important factor of being an expert on your partner.

In my interactions with couples, I have observed maximum human beings don't want their partner to change. They fundamentally recognize their companions as they are. But what humans do need to realize is how to influence, motivate, and otherwise have a superb impact on their partner. They need to keep away from pushing the other's buttons. But that's not sufficient. They also need to recognize the antidotes to apply when matters go awry. They want to be aware of their partner's itch, so they can scratch it for him or her.

In this way, couples are searching to be equipped managers for each other. In fact, their competence as companions isn't always in contrast to the competence of their parents, who want to assuage their baby's painful feelings and cultivate better ones. It also may be compared to the position of a regulator. Partners who're capable managers are capable of helping regulate each other's different moods and excitement levels. As regulators, everyone displays the alternative and is sensitive to jump in and throw a switch to help restore balance in the direction to make the partner feel better. Unfortunately, fear is often the glue holding couples together.

Fear may be beneficial for keeping a companion in line; however, it is glaringly counter to the belief of a pair bubble. We have to want to be within the bubble; we shouldn't feel we ought not to be there. We want to be with our partner because there may be no other area in the world we'd rather be in. Our appeal is primarily based on what we do for each other that no other person can or wants to do. Couples who don't use this type of attraction as their glue are doomed to fail sooner or later.

Exercise: What Can Uplift Your Partner?

Are you privy to what things you can say or do to have the power to relieve misery and uplift your lover? Take a minute and reflect on these now.

1. You may discover the listing of vulnerabilities you made earlier. For each of the three or four matters that make your companion feel bad, you probably can perceive something so one can mollify the bad feeling. For instance, if my history has me doubting my worth as a parent, my partner can predictably brighten my mood with a spontaneous, "You're this type of desirable father," delivery.

2. Check the listing you provided with antidotes, where you might come up with additional ideas.

3. You may want to create a list of the things your companion can do (and does). Do these, please, to uplift you. If you are doing this work collectively, you could create separate lists for each person and then compare notes.

Scratching Your Partner's Itch

Remember how useless Peggy and Simon have been at handling their respective vulnerabilities? Well, that's because it seems they're not better at making each other feel better. As a child, Peggy received tremendous messages about her prettiness, and she usually feels excellent about her appearance. She has questioned her intelligence, however, on every account an instructor humiliated her in grade school. Although Peggy finished college, she regarded herself as a median student.

Simon, on the other hand, has continually considered himself intelligent. Despite his tough upbringing, he managed to put himself through college and earned a degree in chemical engineering. He doesn't consider that he's lovable and profitable as a human being. He never felt actually wanted, and now he always anticipates that Peggy will leave him.

Throughout their European vacation, Simon advised Peggy how stunning she was and how drawn to her he was. Yet he was puzzled why she frequently failed to respond to his compliments and bodily advances. He figured if he just repeated them more frequently, she might be more appreciative. But that didn't appear to work.

Peggy was the one who handles the couple's tour arrangements. Although Simon was aware of her doubts about her intelligence, he by no means employed that expertise by announcing, "You're so smart" or "I love how you know the history of this area" or "I usually learn so much being with you." If he expressed any variation of those messages, he might have experienced a brightening in her face that he saw while commenting on her beauty. This might have resulted in a mutual amplification of fine feelings, as her brightening causes his face to brighten as well. But alas, because he didn't use this technique, he got nothing.

Peggy, on the other hand, sang Simon's praises when it came to his smarts. She surely valued his intelligence and was amazed that the most her remarks get out of him were social smiles. If, however, she looked into his eyes and said, "You are a great man" or "You're the one I've been waiting for" or "I love how you need to keep me close," Peggy and Simon would lose the benefits of a pair bubble. This is the safety and security that includes mutual safety and distress relief, and the power and attractiveness that includes offering the missing vanity portions from adolescence.

As partners, each one holds the keys to the opposite's self-esteem and self-confidence. Remember, as we discussed earlier, shallowness and self-confidence are developed through our touch with other humans. They're now not; they're furnished by the other. That's the way it works and that's how it has usually worked, starting from infancy. Now I'd like you to meet another couple.

Paul and Barbara have become very social because of their remaining child who left the nest years ago. They like going out with friends and enjoy taking part in community and philanthropic activities. Barbara is nonetheless unhappy about the loss of her mother and of her youngsters, who're all away at school. Others might not realize and are not required to recognize, but we actually are. That's our job, and that's why we're paid the big bucks!

We do for our companions what others might now not need to do due to the fact that they don't genuinely care. Of course, our guesses will not be correct one hundred percent of the time. I'm not suggesting you need to be a clairvoyant. It is feasible, for instance, that Barbara's thoughts have moved to an occasion earlier in the day, possibly something she changed into with her husband. In that case, no damage would have come from Paul's incorrect guess; the couple sincerely might have shifted to a brand new topic.

Barbara believes she is unable to address loss, regardless of the reality that she has survived many losses in her life. She has always seen herself as much less appealing than her older sister, who became surrounded with the aid of boyfriends; in contrast, Barbara excelled in academics. Although she knows better as a person, the baby part of her nonetheless believes she was accountable for her father leaving due to the fact she had upset him. This has made the transition of their children from domestic to college even more difficult than it might have been in any other case.

Paul frequently uses his know-how for Barbara's missing pieces and doesn't spend many attempts on matters that have little or no impact on her self-esteem. He often tells her how proud he is of her as a mother and the way he feels about being with her. He keeps reminding her, "Honey, I'm with you for the long haul." He in no way misses a possibility to look at her as though she is the most stunning, sexy girl on this planet and tells her so.

These three or four matters that he gives help heal the past; it supplies her what she most wishes inside the present. He loves that he's capable of healing her emotionally. He scratches the right itch each time. Because of his neglect problems from adolescence, Paul desires to know he is dependent upon and trustworthy. He doubts himself to the sort of degree that he sometimes becomes frozen and unable to stick with the aid of decisions. He wishes to be paid attention to and that his opinion is respected, although he has a manner of undercutting that guide through suspecting that each person who agrees with him is soft-minded.

Barbara makes liberal use of her understanding of Paul's missing pieces and avoids pandering to the things that don't depend on him. She frequently tells him, "I believe you with my life." She never argues with him simply to prove she's proper, however she will turn to him when she believes doing so is vital for both of them. She frequently tells Paul how she believes in his capability to do the proper thing and to restore it if he discovers any other case. Barbara is aware that Paul wishes to shore up his self-esteem and self-worth, and she does it without hesitation because it advantages her.

Barbara and Paul preserve a loving couple bubble. As experts on each other, they can discover when the other has an itch, and they recognize precisely the way to scratch it to provide relief. Often it takes just a smile, a look, or a grasp of the hand to calm each other's primitives and say the words that are needed. They get their wishes met in ways that would no longer be possible if they were by themselves; they do this because they can and because it makes them more appealing — or even indispensable — to each other.

Exercise: The Emote Me Game

You can play this game together with your accomplice, each taking turns to "emote" the opposite. Or you may exercise it without telling your partner what you're doing. Either manner, you stand to learn a lot more when you're dating.

1. Drawing upon your information of your partner, attempt to count on what will cause a grin on his or her face, then watch and notice if it works. For example, you would give your accomplice a rub or relate a uniquely shared memory.

2. Now say something complimentary to your lover to profoundly warm him or her. You will understand you've succeeded if you cause tears to your come to your partner's eyes. I don't suggest tears of sadness, however, the moistness that comes when we feel

deeply touched. Brief, declarative statements are most likely to succeed. Long, drawn-out statements will fail. Avoid adding qualifications. For example, your accomplice may be moved if you say, "You're the most trustworthy person I know," but pronouncing, "You're a totally trustworthy person…most of the time" is unlikely to supply the desired effect. Neither will a lazy compliment, which includes, "You know how I like your cooking." That isn't very moving if you're simply repeating what you believe your accomplice already knows. And don't anticipate immediate results. If your partner doesn't reply to a compliment, take that as statistics about what impacts him or her and attempt something else.

3. Finally, say or do something that causes your partner to get excited. You can see exhilaration in the eyes: they widen and the pupils dilate, if only for an instant. Your baby's face may emerge as redder, and his or her vocal tone may also end up higher in pitch and louder.

4. In each case (whether you're finding a way to make your partner smile, complimenting him or her, or exciting him or her), if you are playing this game

together, don't ask your partner what is going effective. It's your job as the expert to figure this out. And don't ask your partner if what you said worked. Look for the clues; be aware of your partner's reaction. Through this system, you build your knowledge and your partner does the same. You will each receive benefits. Remember, you are wired together! Both of you could play the Emote Me Game every time you feel like it. Experiment with distinct superb effects: make your partner relax; make your companion laugh or something else you could think of.

Fourth Guiding Principle

The fourth precept in this eBook is that companions who're experts on each other recognize how to please and soothe each other. This method becomes familiar with your companion's primary vulnerabilities and understanding their antidotes.

What You Can Do to Help Your Partner

Here are some supporting ideas to guide you in soothing and eye-catching your partner:

1. Learn to unexpectedly repair the damage. Being a professional on your companion means you're usually alert to his or her temper and emotions. If your partner is bothered, you know it immediately. It doesn't matter whether or not your partner is bothered because of something happening between the two of you or due to something outside the relationship. In both cases, you're an expert who can promptly make an educated guess about which of his or her three or four awful things has been touched off. There is not any reason to let any issues fester. Seeing your companion in distress should be the signal to "stop the presses" earlier than moving on with anything else. For example, in case you think you brought on your companion's pain, you would possibly say, "That didn't move well, did it?" or "I'm so sorry. Did that simply harm you?" The worst factor you could do is forget about what you see on your accomplice's face or listen to your partner's voice. Let your partner recognize he or she can anticipate you to step up and say or do whatever is needed to restore the damage. And the same applies to you. You can depend on your partner to be there for you, to recognize your vulnerabilities, and to soothe you while you're upset. It's as though when you shaped your relationship, you took out a contract that would make sure your comfort each other, and now because you've kept up together with your

premiums (this is through being there for your partner), you're able to loosen up each time something seems to be out of hand.

2. Prevent problems before they come up. Knowing how to repair harm is helpful, however, it's even higher to anticipate and avoid difficulties. Of course, it won't be feasible to avoid all challenges. Life doesn't happen that way. But as experts, there are lots you and your accomplice can do to delight and preserve each different mood. Rather than waiting until you notice trouble brewing, be proactive with your accomplice. Make an action of announcing and doing the matters that make him or her experiences desirable. Don't assume your companion already knows all you like about him or her; express everything you admire about your partner. Find new and innovative methods to convey the three or four matters that make your partner's senses accurate. In this manner, you're making deposits that you may draw on when the going gets rough.

3. You may be thinking, what if my lover and I disagree about what our three or four bad things and three or four appropriate things are? The solution is that it doesn't truly need to be counted. It isn't vital that you agree on your personal three or four things or understand the way to scratch your own itch. What's crucial is understanding the

way to do these things along with your partner and vice versa.

So, how do you already know if what you've provided for your companion truly works? The evidence will usually be visible on your companion's face, audible in his or her voice, or apparent in his or her spontaneous shift in mood. There's no need to get right into a debate together with your companion about what your three or four things are. That's why I mentioned this information as a "secret" superpower. Simply reply according to what you recognize as those good and bad things are, then return and watch the results. If it turns out you're no longer seeing the preferred results, chances are you are not yet scratching the right itch. In that case, it's time to go to the drawing board and learn more about your man/woman.

Through a method of experimentation of trial and error, you could retain a higher professional autonomy as opposed to mutuality.

Implicit to Jenny's and Bradley's narrative is a notion is how they see themselves as individuals first and as a pair second. When push comes to shove, they prioritize their personal wishes over their needs as a pair. If you questioned them about this, they may reply that they are "their own man or woman" and don't let the other one boss them around. However, it's not as simple as that.

Yes, everyone expects the opposite to act in a self-reliant fashion, however, in reality, that is the case that suits his or her own reasons. This couple's feelings of independence work especially poorly in situations where they depend upon each other to feel crucial and included. They are ignorant of this trouble when they're maintaining their so-called autonomy, however, they're painfully conscious of it while they experience what may be feelings of neglect.

I think it's fair to mention the autonomy implied by way of Jenny's and Bradley's behavior isn't sincerely autonomy at all. Rather, they are residing to an, "if it's right for me, you should be all right with it" sort of agreement. As a result, they constantly play out situations where they fail to recall the other person. Their underlying message is, "you do your thing and I'll do mine" element.

Sounds mutual, doesn't it? Yet it's miles away because as it requires the alternative partner to be okay. It condones the partners to simply throw one another beneath the bus. In contrast, Bram and Greta seem to recognize something about how the alternative thinks and feels and everyone cares about that. We can say their version is one of mutuality. It is supported by sharing and mutual respect.

Neither expects the other to vary from who he or she is, and both use this shared know-how as the way to shield each other privately and also in public settings. For instance, Greta anticipates Bram's pain and addresses it in a manner that protects his dignity. She acts as though she needs him, though she knows he's the needier one at some point in this situation. Neither Bram nor Greta is poised to throw the other underneath the bus. It is as though they maintain a protective bubble around themselves.

The couple bubble can be a period I choose to use to explain the jointly constructed membrane, cocoon, or womb that holds and protects every partner from the outdoor elements. A few bubbles are an intimate environment that the partners create and preserve together which implicitly ensures such matters as:

"I will never leave you."

"I will by no means frighten you purposely."

"When you're in misery, I'm able to relieve you, even though I'm the only one who's causing the misery."

"Our courting is more important than my need to be right, your performance, your appearance, what humans suppose or want, or the alternative competing value."

You are going to be the primary to pay attention to something and the sensation of closeness is subjective; that's, how close you're feeling to your accomplice and the safe way you're feeling both manifests within you. You will sense getting ready to your partner, but he or she isn't likely to understand how you're feeling unless you say so. Therefore, the same goes for the manner your companion feels about you. Now, discover a number of the ways you provide closeness to your partner:

1. Within the preceding section, I listed some things couples should supply to one another — for instance, saying, "I will never leave you." What have you ever given to your accomplice?

2. What guarantees could you wish to provide?

3. What guarantees could you wish to obtain?

4. You haven't acquired a guarantee from your accomplice earlier. Search for moments as soon as you could be specific with your emotions of closeness and promises of safety.

How Couples Come to Value Autonomy Over Mutuality

Besides our cutting-edge Western emphasis on autonomy, we see increasing proof of loneliness inside and outside of marriages; a rising occurrence of violence and alienation; and divorce rates that, while they will be decreasing, remain well above ideal. Like Jenny and Bradley, couples in distress too frequently deal with solutions that allow you to be summed up with the aid of, "you do your thing and I'll do my mine" or "you look out for yourself and I'll look out for myself."

We pay attention to pop psychology pronouncements like, "I'm no longer able to be at some point of a relationship" and "you want to love yourself before anybody else can love you." Is any of this proper? Is it honestly viable to love yourself before a person ever loves you? Accept it as truth. How ought this be true? If it were, children would inherit this international self-loving or self-hating. And we understand they don't. In fact, citizenry doesn't start by thinking about them, exact or horrific. We discover ways to like ourselves exactly due to how we've experienced being loved by someone. We discover ways to require care for ourselves due to the fact someone has taken care of us.

Our self-worth and shallowness are developed due to humans. If you don't believe what I'm suggesting, check it out for yourself. Recall a time you had when you were younger and your mother and father didn't trust in you. Were you wanting to agree with yourself? Maybe you did. But if so, how did you do it? From wherein or from whom did you get your perception?

Or keep in mind an ex–romantic partner who didn't agree with you or consider you. Were you ready to accept it as true yourself nonetheless? In every one of those cases, chances are that if you did trust yourself, that perception originated with someone important to you. This is how we become as we are: all our earlier interactions and relationships have shaped the person we are today.

Many couples share diverse beliefs of love relationships, but their prior experiences of affection don't match with their ideals. That's a drag, due to the fact personal records constantly trump ideals. That is just the way we're wired. If, for instance, we didn't witness devotion in our mother's and father's marriage, we won't have nice role models for loving to follow in our own adult relationships. Our couples illustrate this precept. Neither Bradley nor Jenny is doing something radically distinctive from what he or she experienced as a child.

Why Pair Up?

You'll possibly be thinking whether the form of commitment I'm suggesting is one you would really like to form. There may be nothing inherently better about coupling than about being single. This ebook is not about what's best, one lifestyle, or a coupled lifestyle. I do understand many perfectly satisfied singles who neither feel the need to avoid coupling nor weep about being uncoupled.

Courting takes time to develop. That is probably super, and if not now, that is probably dandy. Moreover, research on the relative merits of relationships didn't yield company conclusions one way or the other. Some data — inclusive of statistics popularized via authors Linda Waite and Maggie Gallagher of their ebook The Case for Marriage (2000) — advises that married people are happier and healthier than non-married people. However, others — Aloes Stutter and Bruno Frey (2003) in Germany and Richard Lucas and Andrew Clark (2006) within the US — have pronounced that folks who get married tend to be happier in the first area than people who don't marry.

Janice Kiecolt- Glaser and her colleagues (2005) found unhappily married folks to be more vulnerable to illness than people who are happy single parents. This intuition is embedded in our DNA to ensure the survival of our species. However, pairing up for this cause doesn't necessarily translate into the necessity for a long-time period. There's really no proof, at least as far as our species is concerned, that monogamy is nature's mandate. I find it thrilling that a few mammals, like wolves and prairie voles, do pair up for all times. In truth, neurobiologists analyzing voles document that prairie voles (who bond with a partner for life) and meadow voles (who don't bond for life) have identifiable genetic differences. It is viable scientists will one day identify the human genes that designate why we do or do not decide to pair up.

In the meantime, to recognize the reason for pairing up with another human being, we will think about what takes place with a child. The child feels loved and stable, therefore the caretaker also enjoys the feeling of being cherished, and of being with and being concerned for the baby. They are together collectively. We call this primary attachment dating, because the toddler and caregiver are bonded, or attached, to one another. You could say that it is often an "infant bubble" — very much like the couple bubble -- occurring in the course of infancy. If at an early age we are skilled in safety and have a love we ought to believe, and we take this with us. As adults, we are equipped to shape new primary attachment relationships.

On the other hand, if at an early age our relationships with caregivers were less than secure, and the caregiver did not appear to tend to be with us over all different matters, we're probably anxious or involved entering into or being in relationships.

We Come First

Obviously, we will change what came about when we were infants. However, if the early impacts are affecting how we experience relationships now, if they restrict our capacity to shape the forms of bonds we need in our lives, we can move in the direction of resolving them. For some couples, therapy is helpful to achieve this sort of rewiring. Other couples are equipped to talk about and manage their troubles collectively, with minimal outside input.

Let's examine what it takes to create a couple bubble that you, as companions, maintain with one another safely and securely.

Making the Pact

The couple bubble is an agreement to locate the connection before something else. And it means your partner does the equivalent for you. You each agree to do it for each other. Therefore, you tell each other, "We come first." For the duration of this matter, you cement your relationship. Sometimes people say, "I don't want to commit till I am certain this component that worries me won't be of trouble." I have heard variations of this from both women and men in my years as a couple's therapist. There's no surer way to daunt a possible partner than to suggest he or she is insufficient on the subject of any of these or to insist that companion prove himself or herself before protection is assured. This type of method is doomed to fail.

When partners don't honor the couple bubble and complain they aren't being well cared for, often the cause is that they get precisely what they paid for. Pay for a part of something, and you get a part of something. Now, you would probably argue, "Stan, how will you say I should buy him or her before I recognize whether she or he is good and sufficient?" My answer is that if he or she is at this point not appropriately sufficient, then she or he shouldn't even be a contender. However, this isn't usually the case. I see companions who have cautiously and thoughtfully chosen each other, yet, the fear of troubles that will arise after committing to each other turns into deal-breakers.

Typically, those troubles involve standards, one of us is truly going to be fired.

How to Apply Your Couple Bubble

A couple bubble affords a steady place at some stage in which you and your partner can continually ask one another for assistance, and accept it as true with every experience and share your vulnerabilities. It's your primary manner of help and safety. For instance, each time you and your companion enter social conditions, specifically ones involving tough humans, you'll make an idea beforehand that ensures you'll each be covered through your bubble.

As Greta and Bram did, they work together so you'll figuratively hold hands at some stage in the occasion. By holding hands, I suggest firm contact with each other, tracking each other, and being available at a moment's notice. Accept the connection with eye touch, bodily touch, whispering, hand signals, smoke signals — whatever!

Conspire together about how you'll deal with difficult people. Perhaps you may literally hold arms or sit down next to each other in their presence. We'll further discuss the way to protect your couple bubble later. In the meantime, don't forget that splitting up to affect difficult human beings or conditions leaves you vulnerable. Together, you may be formidable.

Did you like this book, or did you find it useful, up till now?

*Your support really makes a difference! I would be very grateful if you would publish an exhaustive review on **Amazon**. All reviews are read personally so that I can get real feedback and make this book (and the whole series) even better.*

Thanks again for your support!

CHAPTER 3

Remember the Good, Forget the Bad

If your partner tends to remind you of things you have done to injure him or her, chances are your reaction is negative. But does it ever occur to you that you helped create that reminiscence inside the first region with the aid of not doing something to restore it in time? Any severe feeling — positive or negative — that remains in our attention for too long will be transferred into long time period reminiscence.

The ambassadors, considerably the hippocampus, are responsible for changing short-term reminiscences into long-term ones. As a primitive involved with our safety and security, the amygdala ensures we don't forget painful recollections. In this way, grudges are shaped. If you're in it for the lengthy haul, it behooves you and your partner to keep away from creating and maintaining grudges. Do this by permitting your ambassadors to overrule your primitives. Fix your horrific recollections so they come to be precise memories.

Kathleen did this with the aid of insisting Dennis speak with her about his task. If she had allowed it to go whilst he became reluctant to speak, they may each have had bad reminiscences: for Dennis, it would have targeted at the activity itself, and for Kathleen, it might have been from her husband withdrawing from her due to the fact he mired into depression. The concept is to convert awful memories into the right ones before they enter the long-time period of reminiscence as grudges. However, it's feasible to transform an awful reminiscence years later. I'm not suggesting lengthy-standing grudges will disappear with a snap of your fingers, however, if you and your partner are willing to do the work, you can get beyond them.

Exercise: The Gratefulness Inventory

This exercise is derived from Naikan, the Japanese artwork of self-reflection. It can be hard to do, especially if you're a wave, however, it is well worth the effort. Take, a minimum, of thirty minutes to try this exercise.

1. At the pinnacle of column 1, write, "What he/she gave me." List everything your partner has given

you within the week. Be precise and concrete. For example, "He made me pancakes for breakfast yesterday," not "He does the cooking." Don't move on until you've listed everything your companion gave you — even the expected things. The fact is, you receive these, too.

2. At the pinnacle of the following column, write, "What I gave him/her." You can spend less time laboring over this column. Nevertheless, be particular and concrete.

3. Label the last column, "The trouble I gave him/her." You may ask why there isn't a fourth column for the problem your companion brought on you: because you probably already understand this all too well. As with the first column, do this thoroughly. And be honest: whether or not you want to or not, you gave trouble and may have been burdensome to your partner.

4. Now study your completed inventory. If you did it correctly, the first and 3rd columns should be longer than the second one. Notice especially what you receive from your companion, but generally tend to take for granted.

5. You may find yourself inclined to write down a letter of gratitude for three matters your partner gave you. You might even feel forced to jot down a letter of apology for three things you probably did to move your partner to grief. And finally, you might need to share this complete listing with your loved one. If all is going well, your companion may want to do the same in return.

Eighth Guiding Principle

The eighth principle in this e-book is that companions who need to stay together need to learn to fight well. When you and your partner are relating within a strong and stable couple bubble, fights don't threaten your partnership. You can detect each other's misery cues and manage them posthaste. You don't ignore issues and allow them to fester. Rather, you are quick to correct errors, repair them, or wave the flag of friendliness.

A few principles to assist you:

1. Losing is not allowed. Of course, no one wants to lose. I'm sure you and your lover are not exceptions. At times, it may be tempting to assert your will, to try to select up a few wins for yourself.

But honestly, what value will your past have if a fight affects your partner being knocked out, on tilt, or otherwise non–compos mentis? Not a good deal. That might be a Pyrrhic victory. So, you need to retrain yourselves. You should rewire your way of fighting. Think in terms of defusing struggle that turns ugly, in place of always resolving it entirely. Most importantly, while you combat, each of you needs to win…or you'll both lose. And that's no longer an acceptable outcome.

2. Giving up isn't allowed, either. Let me be clear: smart fighting is not about relinquishing your role or giving up your self-interest. It's about wrestling with your partner, enticing without hesitation or avoidance, and at the same time being willing to loosen up your very own grip. You go back and forth, till the two of you give something that's good for both of you. You take what you each can bring to the table, and with it, create something new that gives mutual relief and pleasure.

3. Every fight brings a brand new day. In asking you to fight well, I'm asking your ambassadors to rule over your primitives. We all understand that it can be tough, and even more so during a struggle. Don't

anticipate one hundred percent fulfillment on your first try. If the minute a verbal exchange overheats, you forget about the whole lot, at least try not to supply any more fuel to the fire.

Each morning, you look in the mirror and recognize who is staring back at you. Rather than having to always rediscover yourself — the high price on books you gained knowledge of, or your preference for vanilla ice cream — you simply realize who you are. This is your identification, and you depend on it to aid you each day just as you rely upon the ground below your feet. When you're not confident about essential elements of your identification — as is often the case with anxiously attached people — it results in self-doubt. In addition, the more you become aware of issues of your persona, the greater stimulated you are to interpret your moves from that angle and then maintain and behave accordingly. As a result, your self-doubt or sense of inadequacy can overpower you into being indecisive and self-deprecating. Although your perceptions and moves leave you feeling, you preserve the cycle because it leads you into a secure sense of being able to understand yourself and what you think you want from others. It is equally vital that you have an experience of predictability about the identities of other human beings.

Imagine what it would be like to have no idea of whether someone you meet is the equal of Mother Teresa or Jack the Ripper. And people tend to maintain ideals of others, rightly or wrongly, based on certain characteristics — man or woman, Caucasian or Hispanic, white-collar or blue-collar worker, and so on. On an even more primary level, all of us have beliefs about human nature. For example, a few consider that humans tend to be altruistic, whilst others believe that most people they meet are self-centered. Such ideals affect the manner we approach all relationships — from informal to intimate ones.

For instance, you would in all likelihood invite a new friend to your home sooner if you are someone who believes that humans are essentially kind in place of being someone who tends to doubt people's integrity or trustworthiness. The need to view yourself and others in a selected manner is particularly important in terms of your attachment style because that is the fundamental way in which you interact with the world. Your brain "helps" you by offering a picture based on your particular style of what you to look for in your partner and yourself. It only takes a small quantity of evidence to convince yourself that your attachment-related preconceptions are accurate, whether or not they're accurate or adaptive.

For example, there's Jenny, who has a preoccupied type of attachment. She feels inadequate, so she expects her boyfriends will become tired of her and then cheat. Even with her cutting-edge boyfriend, Brian, who frequently expresses his love and regularly tries to reassure her of his dedication, she cannot give up her powerful need to shield herself from any viable abandonment. Whilst he showed up late for a date, she at once interpreted it as a signal that he was hiding something — possibly courting with another female. To her, this turned into additional evidence that she had become useless and unlovable.

Psychologists use the term confirmation bias to describe the tendency of humans to discover reasons to confirm their own ideals. When human beings use this bias to verify what they already think about themselves (appropriate or horrific), psychologists call it self-verification (Swann, Stein-Serous, and Giesler, 1992). These processes are mostly out of focus, so humans can't see how their ideals cause them misery. It's these unseen biased perceptions where people tend to repeat old patterns even if those styles cause pain and failure. However, humans now and again become so unhappy with their lives or relationships that they begin to believe their biases — establishing the opportunity for change.

For instance, Jenny had cried over many unsuccessful relationships. She sensed that Brian had become a "keeper," so she did some sincere soul-searching. She admitted to herself that her fears of Brian leaving her did not make her feel accepted in his steady caring and faithfulness, but she started to censure and undertake those fears. Though it didn't come easily and took a conscious effort on her part, Jenny increasingly became open and trusting of Brian. Ultimately, she began to feel loved — after all, if someone could love her, then she must be worthy of love.

For folks that experience attachment-associated anxiety, opening up to the possibility that they are worthy of love is vital. Challenging your tendency to self-verify and examine your life with a confirmation bias is hard, to say the least. However, you could begin the process by gaining knowledge of what to search for in yourself. It's natural to suppose that you could change your style of interacting by just searching for self-affirmation — for instance, by noting when you are unnecessarily self-critical or recognizing when you unrealistically worry about rejection.

While there may be some basis in this, it's crucial to recognize that such observations may be unsettling or worse. You might resist considering your observations or just have a feeling of something not being proper. You are, in all likelihood, critical of those new, better observations in preference to questioning your preconceived biases. The purpose is that they provide an attitude that demands reassessing situations the very basis of which is the way you feel about yourself and your courting. As a result, they also upset your experience of consolation and safety in the world. However, the more you can understand your biases, the easier it will be to open up to — and search out — a more objective attitude. Slowly you'll start to see yourself and your partner differently.

As referred to earlier, humans are inspired to verify their self-perceptions of being worthy or unworthy of love. They self-verify by selectively paying attention to, selectively remembering, and selectively interpreting statistics (Swann, Rentfrow, and Guinn, 2003). Note how those three principles overlap, and all result in the same way:

Selective interest: People pay greater attention to and spend more time considering comments that confirm their feelings of their personal lovability or unlovability than comments that don't confirm it.

Selective memory: People generally tend to take into account feedback that confirms their sense of being worthy or unworthy of love. Sometimes their system doesn't even record what conflicts with their preconceptions, permit it for themselves or take it into account over the years.

Selective interpretation: People tend to unquestioningly accept as truth that which confirms their sense of being adorable or unlovable. They assume any remarks that conflict with their preconception is because of a mistake or deception. They additionally interpret absent or ambiguous proof as help for their self-perceptions.

As a person who struggles with attachment-related tension, you may notice that you selectively verify that you are not worthy of love within the following way: you attend to any evidence that you are needy, weak, or mistaken in a few manners; and you downplay or fail to see your strengths or fine attributes. Then you recollect matters your partner has stated or completed that seem to confirm that you are inadequate or false in a few critical manners, or that he has, in all likelihood, rejected or left you.

Meanwhile, you fail to keep in mind the times that your partner instructed you of how great you are or stood with you through a tough time. If you aren't in a courting, you have probably not forgotten all of the times you've been rejected, however, you've failed to reflect or consider your loss of interest in others who have been interested in you, or the number of relationships you have enjoyed even though they ultimately didn't pan out. It can be hard to gain enough distance to look at those biases and their results in your daily interactions. So if you want to, spend a while reviewing and applying this section, along with the following exercising, to your life.

Exercise: Observe How You Self-Verify

Review the evaluation of your degree of attachment-related tension in the section "The Basics of How You Connect". This will display your sense of your worthiness of affection. Answer the next questions to help you better recognize the way you hold your self-notion of being unworthy of love (to the quantity which you do sense this manner). It's a crucial step closer to breaking the cycle.

Complete it in terms of your partner, in addition to different people in your life. Repeat the exercise each day until you've got an organic awareness of those problems as you go through your days. Because the pressure to self-verification could make this tough to do, write out your solutions in a manner to stay targeted, and monitor yourself. Hold directly to them to assist in completing and exercising into the next section. You might also find it helpful to talk with a supportive companion or person you trust.

Challenging Selective Attention

What happened during the day that confirmed to you that you are worthy of affection, or that, at the least, brings into question your self-perception of being unlovable? Pick one or two situations (for instance, your partner wanted to watch TV together, or a chum phoned you).

How did you feel in these situations? (For instance, happy, uncomfortable, confused, nothing.)

How did you reflect on these situations? For instance, did you dismiss or reduce this feedback? Did you doubt the honesty or competence of the man or woman giving it? (For example, did you count on your partner wanting to look at TV with you primarily out of habit?)

Can you spot how you are — or might be — self-verifying with selective attention?

Challenging Selective Memory

- What good or nice things did you do today? (Everything counts; nothing is too insignificant)

- In what ways have family members, friends, or maybe buddies proven that they admire you?

- •In what ways did your partner show that he or she cares about you?

Challenging Selective Interpretation

- If you observed that a person has shown you in a few ways that you are unlovable, could you be misinterpreting the other man or woman's motivation or intentions? (For instance, did you misperceive his tiredness as you being uninteresting or unlovable?)

- Could you be making the remarks worse than intended? (For instance, wondering if you're flawed and unlovable while your partner was just attempting to talk about something that disappointed him)

- Are you downplaying your strengths and that you don't live up to your unrealistic expectations or the achievements of your companion and others?

Consider your responses in each section on the topic of tough selective interest, memory, and interpretation. Note how you self-verify yourself in these methods. What topics do you notice? For instance, you might end up effortlessly or constantly getting ready to be rejected; or frequently point out to yourself that you are inadequate, improper, or not as desirable as your companion. You may also struggle with wondering how your partner will stop loving you once he sees the "real" you. Or you might feel disappointed if you interpret your partner as seeming to no longer care about you.

Write down, in detail, the subject(s) which you play out, and maintain this to use within the workout "Revealing Your Invisible Known" in the subsequent chapter. Just as people unconsciously use confirmation bias to self-verify how worthy or unworthy they feel, they also use it to keep themselves emotionally unavailable to their partners (in addition to others). Clearly, people that are preconditioned to assume that others won't be there for them will generally tend to see their partners as emotionally unavailable. So they see themselves as basically alone, and they defend themselves through being self-reliant.

What's less obvious — and seemingly paradoxical — is that you can enjoy yourself alone even when you believe that others are emotionally available. This is likely to take place if you have doubts about whether you're worthy of affection, leaving you to think that those available others ultimately will reject you. So even though you might think positively of your partner at the start of your dating, these perceptions will likely flip negatively over the years, as you discover ways to verify that he really isn't there for you after all. Because of your preconceptions about your partner's unavailability to you, it's possible to assume that an intricate behavior on your lover's part is due to a personality trait that won't change, as opposed to affecting one of a state of affairs or context.

For instance, if your partner doesn't say what he's going to be doing later, you may leap to the conclusion that it's due to a lack of caring, or even to a greater malicious cause of gambling with your emotions — rather than the likelihood that he became in particular busy at work. The more anxiously attached you are, the more likely this is to take place while you are in a terrible mood. This will show up less while you are feeling well or are essentially happy in your dating.

By contrast, when you have a rather avoidant partner, he will think this way even when he is feeling emotionally strong and your dating is going properly. The bias in the direction of seeing others as emotionally unavailable creates "blind spots." You truly don't "see" how you keep your notion that your partner is unavailable. Just as with self-verification, your bias does this through selective attention, selective memory, and selective interpretation — however, this time, it's more the opposite direction.

Every time Dick sees Jane around the house, he ridicules her. Every time Jane sees Dick, she attempts to avoid him. Dick stokes his feelings of superiority by ridiculing Jane. Jane's avoidance reinforces Dick's feelings of superiority. Every time Jane sees Dick, she tries to avoid him. Every time Dick sees Jane, he ridicules her. Jane stokes her emotions of inferiority via keeping off Dick. Dick's ridicule reinforces Jane's feelings of inferiority. Partners keep a balance between them that they both face up to changing, even if the relationship is strained. Each person reinforces his or her self-view by way of behaving in a manner reinforcing it.

This behavior elicits responses from the opposite partner that confirms this self-notion. With such remarks as "proving" what they already "understand" about themselves, human beings once more act in step with their self-perceptions…it's a closed-loop. Bizarrely, the above sample of interaction offers each Dick and Jane an experience of safety — they realize what to expect from themselves and each other, and the way to respond. This predictability affords a comfort even for Jane — how much more difficult would it be for her if Dick was truly superior and in other times nasty? And believe how complicated and uncomfortable it might be for Jane — even though it additionally felt right — if Dick dealt with her continuously nicely when she deeply believed that she was unlovable and anticipated him rejecting her at any moment.

When others deal with you in a way that suits your self-perception, you experience the relationship as feeling effortlessly familiar, even though it's miles apart. You also are much more likely to maintain the connection than if the individual no longer appears to "get" you. For example, as you may anticipate, those who feel right about themselves want to be around others who think highly of them. However — and this is perhaps not as intuitive — nerve-racking humans with low self-esteem regularly leave while their partners persist in viewing them as valuable and cute. Instead, they generally tend to live with and marry much less supportive companions — which reinforces their feelings of being unlovable. There are those in a situation where they may be imprisoned or under social pressure to live in a dating situation that is bad for them. Because such predictability is comforting, any adjustments in a relationship — even positive ones — are regularly met with resistance.

People experience pulls through themselves, in addition to their companions and others, to go back to more predictable approaches. Although this draws to old styles, humans can carve new ones. When someone does change, a few old relationships accommodate to the trade, others die off, and new relationships develop from the "new self." Recognizing and accepting this beforehand can ease the transition.

A right instance of this turned into the film Pretty Woman (1990). I'm not speaking about the title character, but of, Edward (Richard Gere), a sturdy, capable, and extremely successful businessman whose technique of life is coldly calculating. When he meets a girl, Vivian (Julia Roberts), she challenges him to open up. He resists at first, preferring to hold on to his more distant persona. But with time and the new emotionally intimate relationship, he becomes a warmer man. Then he starts to approach his life more humanely.

These adjustments wreak havoc. His legal profession rails against this change, and the other "suits" that work for him balk. But in grand Hollywood style, the target audience is left to accept as true that Edward is a changed man. He marries the girl who has changed him, and his employees should learn to adjust to the brand new him or find a new job.

One of the most usual difficult relationship patterns is the pursuit withdrawal sample, which emerges between an anxiously attached partner (especially for a woman) and an avoidant companion. In reality, it's not so unusual that there's a precise danger that you've experienced it at some point. It works like this: each time the tense accomplice steps ahead or leans in for closeness, the avoidant partner pulls back, which prompts the tense partner to try to get close once more.

Sometimes it can be tough to watch this dance of intimacy below normal topics, discussions, and interactions. To get a feel of how this plays out, do not forget Lucy and Ken. After courting for about a year, they moved in together. Unfortunately, within a few months, their courting ended up more and more strained:

Lucy: When you come home, you barely even say hi to me.

Ken: Well, I'm tired and barely have the strength to simply breathe. But after I've settled in, I do ask you about your day, and you provide me with the cold shoulder.

Lucy: Sure, you come down after having showered, changed clothes, and relax. Meanwhile, I'm stressing out

131

getting dinner on the table for us. You never even offer to help. I get domestic from long hours before you, so I'm tired, too.

Ken: (weakly) I've attempted to help, however, you don't even like how I set the table.

Lucy: You call what you do setting the table? Dropping a napkin and fork close to our chairs rarely qualifies. I need to set it again and refold the napkin and reposition the fork on it. You do the whole thing like that — halfway — after which I even have to complete it up.

Ken: (shrugs his shoulders) No matter what I do, you're never satisfied.

Lucy: I simply wish you'd perform little matters round the place unprompted by me and finish what you start. How tough is that? But you don't, and I end up having to do the whole lot by myself — like the laundry and cleaning up and even planning our vacations. You say you like me, but I don't feel it anymore. I just experience it all by myself.

Ken: (matter-of-factly) Well, I promise to do a better job setting the table; and I'll do more laundry, too.

Doesn't sound very promising, does it? Interestingly, they both suppose they're working on the connection, however…like Lucy, you may get caught in this pattern, focusing on either trying to feel connected or on feeling a lack of connection; every now and then. And so you protest against your partner's distance. Lucy does this by using annoying attention and responsiveness. But her avoidant partner's distance reinforces her experience of not being loved and she worries that she isn't always worthy of affection. Desperate, she does all she can to fight for her relationship, which includes making many concessions to her lover but additionally making frantic demands for increased responsiveness from him.

Their interactions make her feel lonely and enhance her bad feelings for him and their courting (for examples, see the table that follows). Steeped in her emotions, she does not understand his distress in response to her demands.

Or maybe you're more like Ken. An avoidant person stuck in this sample specializes in trying to keep an emotionally secure distance and to stonewall his companion's anger or disapproval. Ken is more cushy when he's impartial and in a powerful — no longer vulnerable — role with Lucy. When she turns to disillusion, he tries to emotionally distance himself from her feelings and his fears of separation. He does this with the aid of thinking about her in a negative way (for example, see the table). He also withdraws, turning more strongly to his inclination to be self-reliant. In doing this, he fails to understand or recognize Lucy's bids for closeness, warmth, and reassurance; or how his lack of emotional expressiveness and shortage of heat makes her experience painful.

The maximum common long-term sample for these couples is that both companions grow to be more severe in their positions. However, for many of them, there may be a subsequent flip in their roles.

Over the years, the avoidant man or woman becomes more remote and antagonistic; and the irritating person will become more disappointed and lodges more excessive protest behaviors, consisting of also being adverse or threatening to leave. But among stormy times, the stressful character displays better memories and emotions, continuing to reach out in a more positive, reconciliatory manner.

The avoidant companion, however, remains withdrawn and angry. Gradually, the demanding partner stops trying. Often, in those couples that marry, the wife — who is in all likelihood the aggravating companion — decides to leave after the kids grow up and move out (although she doesn't always wait that long). Taken unawares, the husband desperately pursues her.

Although complex, this is not a very unusual scenario. The pursuit-withdrawal dynamic goes mainly wrong in some relationships, which turns out to be controlling and abusive. A nerve-racking partner may resort to intimidation or aggression to get attention, reassurance, or love from an unresponsive and detached companion. Occasionally, it's the avoidant companion who is aggressive, though this is more regularly passive-aggression — expressed, for instance, in cold silence, rolling eyes, or other methods of being disrespectful. This behavior is the avoidant companion's way of trying to get the worrying partner to move off.

Exercise: What Would a Fly on the Wall See in Your Home?

It may be very enlightening to take note of the styles of conversation for your dating — especially the ones related to conflicts. Noting the emotions, thoughts, and moves of each party can help to provide critical insights. Consider the following example: Jill feels hurt that Paul doesn't spend time with her on the weekends and prefers to hang out with his friends. She thinks he doesn't care. She expresses this by crying and telling him he's selfish. Paul feels attacked, thinks she is overreacting and reacts by withdrawing. Jill feels hurt, and the cycle repeats.

With this in mind, think of a struggle that tends to repeat in your dating. Now recall the next questions partnered with it. (Although those questions expect that you are the one to start the dissatisfaction, you can regulate them to deal with your partner starting the disagreement). As the conflict continues:

FEELING: How do you feel while this is happening?

THOUGHT: How are you considering your partner?

ACTION: How do you specify the problem?

FEELING: What do you imagine your partner is feeling on the receiving end?

THOUGHT: What do you think your partner is thinking about you?

ACTION: How does your partner respond?

Note how the interaction happens and how it ends (for instance, there is an explosion; or both of you withdraw). For the questions about your partner, it is helpful to ask your companion what he would be feeling and thinking — however, you could talk about this productively with him.

Otherwise, try empathizing to assume his responses; or ask someone you agree with for help.

Review Your Patterns

- How do you and your partner affect each other's feelings and actions?

- What styles do you notice?

- How does this interaction reinforce your beliefs about how worthy of love you are?

- How does this interaction make your ideas stronger about how emotionally available your partner is?

At an appropriate calm time, you might want to talk along with your partner about this exercise, sharing the insights it's given you. You might also ask your companion how the interactions affect his sense of being, worthiness of love, and feelings of emotional availableness. There is a lot to make sense of inside yourself, in addition, to attempt to work out with your partner. This is an area which you would possibly find useful to spend some time reviewing. You might also find it useful to go through this now, then refer back to it again at a later time.

In this section, I have proven how your attachment style, self-verification, and affirmation bias keep you repeating old patterns. They distort your perceptions and frequently assist counterproductive methods of viewing yourself and your companions (past, present, and future). That's a lot to try to absorb. To completely get it, you should spend some time turning it over in your mind. Apply it to the way you've lived your life and continue to do so.

In the following chapter, I lay out how it's feasible to recognize all of these records in a summary and still be unaware of your tricky approaches to interacting within the world. This understanding can help open your eyes to ways that set up happier, healthier relationships. While people are aware of their relationship patterns and are motivated to change, they often unconsciously undermine their attempts at self-improvement. For instance, Vito loved Miranda and knew that his distrust (unjustified) dissatisfied her. He worried that he would drive her away, so he dedicated himself to placing belief in her, specifically after she yelled at him for snooping on her mobile phone.

One week later, he suddenly picked up Miranda's cell phone to see if she had been texting other guys. With her in the next room, this conduct was regarded as blatantly self-destructive, but that did not change the rationale. This happened at some point after he noticed a former girlfriend holding the hand of a man at the mall. Though inaccurate and risky, his quick peek at Miranda's Smartphone turned into his try to help himself regain a sense of safety.

As I've noted, people want a sense of security in each day's life. The power to discover is far heightened while you are scared of losing your companion. This can cause you to experience the equal primal panic you might have felt as an infant, when every chance threatened your survival and how you desperately searched for your mom and dad to console and protect you. In other words, while you sense that your partner may not be there for you, you may feel — at a core degree — scared to death. Or while you try to trade in ways that struggle with your attachment style, that are designed to hold you safe, you're possibly instinctively returning to your familiar attachment behaviors — even though those behaviors (like Vito's) are counterproductive and fly within the face of your conscious dedication to "do better."

This manner of understanding conduct isn't intuitive and can be confusing. So let's take a closer look. People's attachment styles and attachment-associated behaviors are so much a part of who they are — and may be so strongly influenced by primal panic — that it's extremely hard for them to understand all of the ways by which they self-affirm, even if they understand to look for this bias. Sometimes their bias can be so all-encompassing that it prevents their recognition of problems even when they are glaring. For instance, a few anxiously attached people turn to alcohol as a way to appease their distress after feeling rejected. Even while this dangerous coping crosses the road into alcoholism, they often don't recognize or know the overall quantity of their trouble because it could disappoint them more. Sometimes they remain in denial even after repeatedly being caught driving drunk.

Similarly, many anxiously attached women blame themselves whilst they are verbally abused and beaten by a partner — something that occurs all too often — and continue to choose to live in that dating circle. For the ones on the outside looking in, it is incomprehensible how those struggling can't truly see the troubles and solutions (for instance, just stop drinking, or leave the bastard).

Even more maddening to onlookers is the on-again-off-again acknowledgment of issues. For instance, take into account, Linda. She knows she had "it all" — a loving husband, fantastic kids, no financial worries — however, she changed and became depressed. She became irritated with herself because she didn't think she had any right to be sad. Yet even in our first session, it was clear that she felt her husband didn't admire her, and that she'd dedicated her life to him (and others) so much that she didn't do something for herself — and so she felt deprived.

When I repeated her words to that effect, she responded as if she was hearing it for the first time. "I just said that, didn't I? Wow." But only a few minutes later, she lamented that she didn't know why she was so sad. She virtually did know on a few stages that those struggles existed or she couldn't have instructed me about them. But she also couldn't allow them to reside completely and conveniently in her consciousness. So, in a sense, she knew them but didn't know them.

You revel in this when you feel that something conflicts with your attachment style or demanding situations attached to your identity, yet you don't fully acknowledge it. It's a protective manner of distancing yourself from a psychological danger or emotional pain (a dynamic frequently mentioned by therapists as "dissociation"). You can also get a sense of "knowing-however-now-not-understanding" in this way: consider a person who acquired attention as an infant when she became incredibly emotional. Based on this early experience, she would preserve a sample of being overly emotional with others into adulthood. Although she's privy to being an emotional character, she does not consciously understand that it's her manner of getting close to others — which contrasts with Linda's partial attention of why she became unhappy. I name both of these understanding-however-now not-understanding experiences the invisible recognized. (I have tailored this term from British psychoanalyst Christopher Bollas [1987], who introduced the time period unsought to describe those stories that people don't forget because they originate before the age of 3.)

When you battle with know-how, why is it so hard to change the approaches you act in relationships? Do not forget about your past as a way to tap into the invisible known because patterns are established on preceding reports (with formative years having a robust effect). Human beings now and again respond to present conditions in a way that only makes them feel when one considers their past.

Linda spent her youth attempting to unsuccessfully delight her mom, who handled her harshly. With this statistic, it was not difficult to understand how she evolved a way of being more kind to humans and working hard to avoid their wrath. While her "niceness" helped her to make many friends, it often left her feeling unimportant. Not surprisingly, she struggled with the invisible and changed into being unable to speak to her husband between the many concerns between them — issues that piled up over the years.

Eventually, she became distressed enough to seek therapy. Unfortunately, if you have dangerous ways of coping or regarding others, your attempts to fix troubles and cope regularly end up in a vicious cycle. They make things worse. Linda's state of affairs is a great instance of this. She answered to her fear of rejection by being extra first-class; however, this caused her to feel unimportant and rejected, which she replied to by trying even harder to be better. Similarly, the drinker makes use of alcohol to calm his misery, which results in greater problems and more misery. He responds by again seeking to numb himself with alcohol, thus starting the pattern over again — while his marriage falls aside and his ability to work deteriorates.

And as any perfectionist will tell you, the harder he attempts to get the whole lot better, the greater the problems he sees with his performance. You might wonder, "Okay, I get the big picture, however, why can't people just change as soon as these considerations are pointed out?" This seems logical — like being able to open a safe as soon as you're given the combination. But it's not that easy. The very complexity that enables you to expand your identity, so you can act without any problems in your routine, also makes such simple solutions ineffective. People frequently have conflicting minds or beliefs or get feedback that clashes with their beliefs; and such conflicts cause inner tension that psychologists call cognitive dissonance.

It's an incredibly uncomfortable experience that humans unconsciously go to splendid lengths to avoid. In their ebook, Mistakes Were Made, psychologists Carol Travis and Elliot Aronson explain, "In an experience, dissonance principle is a principle of blind spots — of ways and why people by accident blind themselves so that they fail to notice vital occasions and statistics that could throw them into dissonance, making them question their behavior or their convictions" (2007, 42). To understand how this influences your attachment style and relationships, do not forget that you set up your attachment style to experience security within the world."

This way of being starts to shape in formative years and is strengthened through day by day stories over a life-time of self-verification and confirmation bias — your attempt to prove that you are who you believe you are (for instance, unworthy of affection) and that others are who you believe they are (for instance, to have an attachment).

To clarify, consider an anxiously attached lady with low self-esteem. She may momentarily feel right with her boyfriend complimenting her, however, this may create cognitive dissonance, so she will speedily revert to viewing herself negatively, with an assortment of reasons to rationalize why she's "undeserving" — all of which resolves her dissonance via self-verifying (and reinforcing) her negative self-image. This is how cognitive dissonance and self-verification images block the alternative.

To complicate matters, how human beings experience past occasions can keep them from letting go of these events and motive them to act in dangerous ways or to conflict with positive situations. For instance, the fact that a female intellectually knows that she was sexually abused as an infant does not magically relieve her of the emotional pain from the experiences, any more than knowing that a person hit you over the head with a brick can heal your fractured skull. So she may try to keep away from thinking about those facts at the same time as she maintains feeling uncomfortable with physical intimacy.

In conditions like this, while people are pressured to avoid emotional pain or the motives for it, they're left to exist with the invisible known — which has its own nagging ache — and to blindly repeat problematic behaviors or stories. While it may seem to make sense to propose to yourself to "just let it go; it's in the past," this recommendation is useless. No one wants to feel dissatisfied; believing you are purposely torturing yourself to provide for your pain.

Even those who are usually avoidant and relatively good at denying emotional pain need to deal with the invisible known when it becomes so painful or destructive that they're forced to stand it. For instance, Laura was a live-at-home mother who used her strength of mind to hold shape for her and to assist her to impose shape on her family. However, as her children grew older, they began to resist her control and she started to lose her temper. Their rising independence unleashed her emotions (which she had constantly managed to suppress) and her self-doubts (which she had not often even acknowledged to herself). Her distress made it impossible for her to stay self-reliant and revealed how alone she had felt in her marriage. Somewhere deep inside, she had constantly recognized that she felt distant from her husband and that she had created this divide. The now-you-see-it-now-you-don't invisible made confronting it hard.

To completely know and question it, humans have to persistently assign the rules that they implicitly use, together with looking ahead to others that will certainly love them and be there for them. For instance, Laura turned into able — over the direction of remedy — to acknowledge that she by no means completely depended on her husband to be supportive, so she had commonly brushed off his caring gestures and ideas of how he let her down.

As she risked being vulnerable through sharing this with her husband, she found that he became knowledgeable and also wanted more in-depth courting. By commencing up to experiencing yourself and others differently, you may begin to loosen your corporate grip on the past and heal from it. This allows you to change how you relate to yourself and others in the present.

Exercise: Revealing Your Invisible Known

In the early part of this chapter, you completed the "Observe How You Self-Verify" exercise, which helped you to perceive ways in which you self-verify. Review your answers or complete the exercise again. Now, for this section's exercise, we'll take it a step further. Be aware of a topic or two that you chose to focus on. Read the themes that you diagnosed whilst completing that workout inside the last section. Then reconnect along with your observations of how you self-verified to play them out.

Ask yourself:

- How did you experience this as you challenged your selective interest, selective memory, and selective interpretation (for instance, anxiety and discomfort)?

- How did your bias affect your ideals regarding yourself?

You might realize that you could see your bias, however, you'd lose your attention as you get sucked into the bias itself. For instance, you would possibly see that you tend to push aside your partner's real caring as his simply meeting an obligation as opposed to permitting yourself to understand that your bias keeps you from being open to the possibility of his love and you may get caught up in proving to yourself that he doesn't absolutely love you and that he might go away at any time. Seeing your bias after having it disappear is proof of the invisible acknowledged. It's similar to a magic trick — now you see it, now you don't!

Practice this exercise over and over with different examples of the same subject matter. Repeating it will assist you to become more aware of how your invisible recognized your feelings and behaviors. It will help you to see your part in your dating troubles. It may be very useful and enlightening to share your observations, thoughts, and feelings with someone supportive of your lifestyle — perhaps even your accomplice. Journaling can also assist.

When human beings with an anxious attachment style over performance to show their value, they're often simultaneously trying to cover their worry of rejection, their feelings of insecurity, and other struggles partnered with themselves and others. Each time those issues recur, they're unconsciously shoved into the proverbial closet away from awareness (as mentioned earlier, many therapists refer to this as dissociation).

Eventually, the "junk" (and troubles partnered with it) pushes to come back out — similar to the famous cool animated film of a bulging door of an overstuffed closet. People react to their developing distress in many ways, including experiencing depression, tension, insomnia, widespread fatigue, or persistent back pain. They may also overeat, abuse alcohol, or shop to excess. Even while you may understand intellectually that a selected bias causes you distress, you can no longer pay much actual interest to it. Instead, you revel in an experience of knowing that it's "just the way things are." You might "realize" that you are unlovable, and you might also "recognize" that others won't reliably be there for you.

As Robert Burton (2008) efficiently argued in his ebook <u>On Being Certain: Believing You Are Right Even When You're Not</u>, humans' experience of knowing is beyond what they can manage and can't be effortlessly argued away. It's a powerful pull for them to stay as they've always been, even if they're carrying out self-defeating behaviors. For instance, anxiously attached human beings with low self-esteem can listen to advice on ways to build themselves up; they can assume nice thoughts; they can invest themselves in a mess of ways to experience good — however, all to no avail. To a deep degree, they "recognize" that they are unacceptable in some critical manner. Remember, they evolved their identity over time and it gives them a feeling of protection. But eventually many of them feel a lot of misery that they're compelled to remember that something has to give — although they don't understand what it is.

Even avoidant human beings, who tend to keep an in-manage manner, are every so often pushed out of their consolation zone via intense and chronic stressors. The emotions of being by themselves and vulnerable that they have defended towards their complete lives fail them, and so they're compelled to take care of emotional pain. At those times, they may be willing — if not precisely eager — to try something special. So since it's your attachment style, you are probably going to challenge the status quo most effectively after feeling sizeable distress or emotional pain.

By taking the hazard of truly seeing the difficult modern-day biases of yourself and others, you emerge as free to recollect new perspectives — a tough feat given that the purpose of your attachment style is to preserve the feeling of being secure and sound in the world.

One of my sufferers shared an insightful quote to explain why she ultimately came to me to remedy years of suffering from this battle: "And the day came when the danger to remain tight inside the bud became more painful than the threat it took to blossom." (The supply of this quotation is unknown, although it has on occasion been attributed to Anis Nin.)

Feeling emotional pain and information the way you keep complicated patterns does not inform you how to be extraordinary or robotically set up for healthier patterns. This has to develop over time with new reviews. For example, you could realize that you tend to be guarded with anybody for your current life, even your spouse, because you felt criticized or emotionally deserted as a child by your mom and dad; or because a former fiancé cheated on you with your closest friend. However, even after you recognize this, you still have a few tasks in advance of you in case you need to change. You must permit yourself to let down your defenses and experience vulnerability inside a caring relationship. Then you'll need to develop the inner resilience to keep reaching out even after you feel harm by your new love (as a way to succeed sooner or later in any close relationship).

But there's no reason to stress too much about this. Just proceed slowly. You'll want to feel yourself stretch, but not so much that you snap. To illustrate further, recall Jessie. Her parents loved her; however, they had been by nature incredibly emotionally remote. They would smile and giggle and act out a "normal" family life, but they focused their attention on their kids' achievements in preference to their children's more personal characteristics and studies.

When Jessie and her siblings were sad, harmed, or distressed in any way, her mom and dad order them to stop whining with a pull-yourself-up-through-the bootstraps mentality. Jessie learned how not to complain. She came to consider that her imperfect performance and distressing emotions were not the most effective plan and that she wouldn't be cherished, but she was essentially improper and unworthy of affection.

No one remembered what accomplishments she finished in life (and there had been many); she never felt worthy enough. She usually looked towards others to see her mistakes and see her unworthiness — and reject her. Unfortunately, this also meant that she didn't trust any male who showed interest in her until he changed into rejecting her in a few ways. As you may anticipate, the relationships she had with men had been brief and emotionally painful.

For Jessie, like many of those who are raised in families that make attractiveness contingent on overall performance, being self-vital became a manner of coping that made sense — she sought to fix all the problems in her performance so that her parents would be pleased with her and love her. As an adult, her "overlearned" self-complaint turned into part of her identification that she used to try to assist herself in three vital methods. First, to enhance her overall performance, she could spare herself pain by understanding she changed into much less than perfect and unlovable. Second, she could avoid rejection, which she thought would manifest if she failed in any manner. And her efforts frequently paid off in others' being happy with her overall performance (though she wouldn't allow herself to be completely taken in by this).

When Jessie started her remedy, she was desperate to be free from her self sabotage, however, she couldn't determine how to escape. She changed for a healthier, happier manner of being which did not need a map to get there. To depart from someone's past, beaten-down, and circular paths, you ought to devise an effective escape route (or be helped by someone who has this type of plan). For Jessie, that route was learning to value her entire self, not just what she should accomplish. Once she succeeded in doing this, she became capable of seeing the importance of her self and loosened up to experience her life and relationships. On our paths, as with our lives, "the devil is in the details."

The next chapter will offer a few crucial pointers on how you can broaden a customized escape route.

By this point within the book, you already know your attachment style. You understand what causes you to perpetuate bad and ineffective approaches to seeing yourself and your partner. These are extremely vital insights, but as you grow your self-recognition, you may also sense a sturdy pull to reaffirm your old perceptions of yourself. You'll find ways to continue seeing yourself, your partner, and your dating as you always have, and to face up to the potential recuperation effect of what you are learning.

If you persist, a new perspective will prevail. You could be free to learn how to nurture a happier relationship, and perhaps even change your attachment style. While this offers promise, the billion-dollar question is how to do it — how can you maintain insight into unhealthy patterns and finally nurture a happy relationship? When faced with this question, it's natural for humans to look for direct answers — a listing of fail-safe techniques or approaches for these challenges. They search for concrete tools: do this; don't do that. Often, however, the direct technique fails us. People can't successfully use the "good" advice they're given because their internal environment supports the bad reputation.

What's needed is a way to trade that core environment — a manner that immediately improves the way you relate to yourself and emotionally connect to your companion. This makes me reflect on what befell a small plant as soon as I had it. Its inexperienced leaves gave my workplace a touch of warmth, notwithstanding its loss of flowers. But once I moved to a workplace with a big wall of warm windows that faced the morning sun, purple blooms exploded throughout it and brightened up my office, as well as my mood. Similarly, human beings can get the "sunshine" they need to blossom from loving relationships.

If you are constantly standing within the shadows of your attachment-related anxiety, there are two ways you could bring happiness to your relationships — and even "earn" secure attachment — which I touched on in section 2. One manner is with an emotionally capable attachment who is loving, accepting, and consistently to be had. This may be a romantic partner, but not necessarily so. This figure could be a family member, a friend, a clergy person, a therapist, a mentor, or even God. Really, it can be any person to whom you feel you can turn for support.

The other manner is through what I call compassionate self-awareness — and cognizance of yourself from the attitude of resolving, and a preference to lessen, your suffering. In each case, love seeps in overtime to comfort and reassure you that you are worthy of it. Ultimately, to earn a stable attachment, you need to be open to an emotionally available attachment parent and be open to being compassionately self-aware. Fortunately, a loving companion allows you to expand compassionate self-attention; and compassionate self-focus allows you to be more open to a truly loving partner. Each of these can build on the other — a bit at a time — and will help you become more worthy of love, see your companion in a finer light, and work with your companion to nurture a happy, wholesome relationship.

Additionally, they will let you create a sense (or a greater intellectual representation) of your companion you can deliver with you anyplace you go, which can console and reassure you in times of distress (the couple bubble). The concept that having the right partner allows you to experience cherished memories which is what dreams — and romantic stories — are made of. You can intuitively recognize it.

But compassionate self-conscious desires need explaining. The idea grew out of my gnawing curiosity about what numerous areas of mental literature (not those that I knew of) had to mention about developing personal change. As I plowed through piles of research and meditated on my knowledge, the concept of compassionate self-cognizance presented itself as vitally vital in personal change and recovery. Its main factors are self-awareness and self-compassion, both of which I will explain extensively. Then, I will provide you with detailed information for developing the specific components of this crucial talent set.

Self-Awareness

To improve your intimate relationships, you ought to look at your performance in growing problems — or at what you do to keep your relationships from even getting started. As I've explained, humans' biases generally tend to blind them to these insights. Making effective use of them could be tricky, but in case you persist in observing your tendency to confirm your preconceptions of yourself and your partner (or capability partner), you may see these biases effortlessly and clearly.

No longer mistaking perceptions as absolute truth, you'll be freer to initiate positive changes. It's beneficial to think about self-cognizance as comprised of feelings, consciousness of mind, and internalization. Awareness of emotions offers a richness of experience that would be lacking in a purely intellectual life. It's the distinction, for instance, between knowing a new romantic interest is a superb fit for you on paper and the feeling of being on cloud nine. By focusing on emotions, humans can identify beliefs or experiences that they were previously unaware of, or that they did not recognize the energy of. For instance, a girl could realize she is in love with a friend after feeling pangs from dating someone else. Another instance is a woman who knows she likes spending time by herself but realizes just how critical this is when her new boyfriend becomes clingy.

Emotions don't simply breathe life into existence; they offer information for us to behave on. Along with being in touch with their emotions, people need to self-regulate — or manage themselves —so that they don't become overwhelmed. They attempt to do that in some special ways, many of which fail — and some of which you might relate to. For instance, they may try to suppress, deny, or numb distressing emotions. But if those procedures are used too frequently, the emotions go underground and may resurface at a later time — often with a vengeance, leaving humans anxious, depressed, or angry.

An exclusive approach is when human beings ruminate, repeatedly reviewing the reasons and results of a problem as they search for a solution. But while the problem has no real or clean answer, they stay caught in a cycle of feeling disenchanted and anxious, attempting to remedy the problem and reduce their misery, failing to repair their problem, and then feeling more anxious. Or they become so overwhelmed that each of their feelings feels like one huge boulder sitting firmly on their chest.

By contrast, those who self-regulate successfully are capable of tolerating and dealing with their emotions. They can use the coping strategies stated above, however, they do it without working in opposition to themselves in other ways. For instance, they may suppress their emotions while at work, but permit themselves to become disenchanted at home and speak about their feelings with their partners and others. Because they aren't particularly threatened by their distress, they don't protect too strongly against it. This lets them become fully self-aware. As a result, they can ride the wave of their feelings instead of drowning in them.

To help clarify, recollect someone who is grieving over the death of a close friend. If this man or woman is frightened by or wishes to keep away from his grief, he would possibly shut off his feelings, leaving him caught in emotional numbness (although blanketed from the pain) and unable to hook up with others in a meaningful way. In contrast, someone who is more accepting of grief is normally capable of sharing it with loved ones and maintaining emotionally close relationships. Although struggling with negative feelings is continually painful, individuals who can self-regulate efficaciously do not sense emotional suffering (misery about their misery) as lots of individuals who combat their feelings.

Sometimes human beings assume that acknowledging a difficult state of affairs means that they then need to either be resigned to it or act on it. If they are not prepared to do either, they are denying their feelings. And in the end, they remain distressed without a way to deal with it.

For example, Amelia doesn't want to simply accept that her husband is unkind to her because she fears that she would then need to either leave him, which she isn't prepared to do, or resign herself to being unhappy. Actually, her feelings no longer imply either of these things. They really mean that she is unhappy right now. Once she acknowledges and accepts this, she will be in sync with herself. She may even realize new options — like the fact that she could be happier without him, or that they could work on their marriage together. Of course, she could also decide to surrender herself to the state of affairs; however, she might be doing it with a special state of mind allowing her to consciously decide the best method to stay inside the marriage.

Distinguishing Thoughts and Emotions

It is vital to recognize the distinction between thoughts and feelings. You may be surprised to discover that many human beings confuse them. For instance, it would not be unusual for a person to mention, "I feel like I was too quiet on that date." This, of course, is a concept and not an emotion. Emotions are a combination of being aroused in a particular way and the meanings we position to that arousal. So you may feel embarrassed not speaking a lot on a date.

When people mistake their thoughts for emotions, their real emotions stay unexplored. Simply spotting this mistake, which focuses on emotions, often leads human beings to revel in themselves more emotionally. For instance, as soon as you realize you are being embarrassed, you would also understand that you are afraid of being judged. And then you could seek reassurance or support, or you might recognize that your worry is unnecessary.

To illustrate how negative emotional self-cognizance may be trouble, take into account a scenario that regularly happens in therapy. A woman — let's use the name Maxine — is suffering from her husband's infidelity. She says, "I feel like I can't trust him anymore. And, really, how can I? He might inform me he was at work when he was certainly..." And off she goes, telling me all the awful things he has done. Her speech is rapid and she sounds angry — the more she talks, the more dissatisfied, crushed, and confused she becomes. Despite being emotional, her suspicions and examples of his dishonesty are thoughts, not emotions, so I refocus her on what she is feeling.

With some prompting, she acknowledged feeling indignant, betrayed, unhappy, scared, and hurt. She cried as she connected with all of those feelings, and she felt heard. Despite the cliché of a therapist looking to get patients to cry, my awareness (and the beneficial part of this interchange) is to connect her with her feelings and help her feel heard; crying is simply the inevitable final result of her doing that. Whether or not she wants to plan on resolving her marriage, she is in contact with the pain that desires healing, and so she can begin to work on easing that pain.

Exercise: Opening Up to Emotion

Intertwined with naming your feelings is the way you pick them out. You have to step out of your judgment so one can evaluate them. This stepping out lessens your immersion in your emotions. To assist you, don't forget the way you experience now. Really, please do that properly. I can wait a minute. Notice the way your thought shifted from thinking about focusing on your feelings to being attentive to your emotions to thinking about the label for them. This ability to shift attention can be very beneficial in permitting you to have your emotions while no longer being eaten up by them — especially when they are difficult feelings. The right way to exercise this is with low-depth feelings, which have less of a danger of overwhelming you.

Just as you stopped moments in the past to remember your feelings, make it a practice to try this at different times throughout your day. For example, you may do it at mealtime, before leaving your own home in the morning, or upon arriving at your office. The important point is for you to discover ways to enjoy your feelings — heightening your attention to them, being in them, and consciously looking at them. With practice, you will be better able to do this with more extreme emotions. And the better you are at doing it, the freer you'll be to view your situation from several angles — possibly keeping in mind alternative approaches to recognizing or replying to your scenario. If, like many humans, you have some trouble identifying your unique feelings, don't worry. That's not an unusual problem, and that's one to work out in the next section.

Common Humanity

This is the recognition that anyone shares in commonplace studies, inclusive of pain and suffering, weaknesses, and imperfections. By relating to others in this manner, people feel much less isolated and lonely. They realize that their issues are simply part of being human and that these difficulties no longer imply that there may be something wrong with them. So in preference to being mired in self-pity, those with a sturdy sense of humanity tend to feel greater kindness (although not always happiness) during their struggles.

Mindfulness

This is a nonjudgmental focus of thoughts and feelings without an attachment to them. Unlike the dialogue of cognizance of mind and emotions within the "Self-Awareness" segment above, mindfulness focuses more on the method of cognizance — how you approach and treat your experiences — than on exploring and differentiating the lessons themselves. When you are mindful, you are genuinely inside the moment. You receive results without the need to deny, suppress, or exaggerate them. You also have a perspective for your reviews, more self-compassion, and a greater sense of well-being during demanding times.

The blessings of mindfulness become obvious when you take into account what happens when human beings are not mindful. For instance, people who are effortlessly triggered to feel negativity sense rejection regularly, have a bad attitude and identify poorly with their feelings. They react by being clingy or lashing out in anger. In both cases, they push their partners further away instead of seeking the closeness they sincerely crave. And if they are trying to suppress their terrible feelings, those feelings regularly come again with even more depth. By contrast, if these human beings sought out more mindfulness, they could feel much less beaten, even amid distressing emotions, and could recognize themselves and their reactions better. As a result, they might respond in more healthy, constructive methods including by speaking with their partners about their struggles and directly asking for reassurance (Walling, 2007).

As Neff (2008) emphasizes, self-compassion cannot arise without self-kindness, humanity, and mindfulness. People have to enjoy self-kindness; they need to be influenced to behave on their own behalf towards a feeling of well-being. They must understand and experience that they're part of commonplace humanity in which anyone struggles as they do. And, finally, they need to remember so that they can be aware of their views without being overwhelmed by them.

Together, these three elements can help you to nurture a tremendous experience of yourself, give you a better sense of protection with your partner, and a more powerful manner to deal with troubles in your relationship.

Exercise: What's Your Level of Self-Compassion?

Given the importance of self-compassion in alleviating attachment-related anxiety, you may discover it beneficial to assess yourself in each of the factors that make it up: self-kindness, common humanity, and mindfulness. On a scale of 1-5, assign how properly you become aware of it with the statements in place. Then divide this by the number of statements in each vicinity to get your final score for the section.

Self-Kindness

(Rate Yourself 1-5 for each statement)

- You are accepting and mild with yourself in reaction to your imperfections or inadequacies.

- You are accepting and gentle with yourself when you make mistakes.

- You are concerned and nurturing of yourself while you are hurting or emotionally upset.

- You treat yourself kindly so that you can be happy inside over the long term.

Your Total ÷ four = Your Self Kindness

Common Humanity

- You accept the truth that others have weaknesses, imperfections, or inadequacies just like you do.

- You can see your struggles as part of being human; you realize you aren't on your own in them.

- When dissatisfied, you may forget that other humans sometimes have comparable struggles and emotions.

- Remembering that different human beings have similar struggles and emotions helps you to seem less different from me.

Your Total ÷ four = Your Common Humanity

Mindfulness

- You can accept your thoughts and emotions without judging them — even when upset.

- You can accept your thoughts and feelings without denying, suppressing, or exaggerating them.

- You can revel in your feelings without becoming overly identified with them and dropping perspective.

- When disappointed or throughout difficult times, you try to keep a healthy attitude.

Your Total ÷ four = Your Mindfulness

Your Total ÷ 4 = The better your rating for a region (the highest rating is a 5), the more potent you are in it. Keep those scores in mind while you figure out the main components of self-compassion.

For any areas of weakness, you may select to focus more on the exercises that focus on strengthening them.

Nine Benefits of Self-Compassion

To better recognize the benefits of self-compassion don't forget this example: Dan is at a celebration along with his date, Jill, and her friends. He doesn't recognize an awful lot of artwork, which is what most in their careers or pastimes appear to revolve around. Rather than risk losing Jill's respect by way of saying the wrong thing, he shuts down and doesn't say a word. He relates to his party in a confusion of worry at being seen as incompetent. By contrast, Lucas — who's with his female friend Sophie at the outlet of an art show, though he has little awareness of artwork — isn't worried about being regarded as incompetent. He accepts that each person has strengths and weaknesses. He admits to his confusion about the way to proceed by acknowledging his obstacles. He asks considerate questions, appreciates the insights offered, and feels good about the understanding he gains.

Not surprisingly, Dan wins no allies among Jill's friends, who view him as remote while Lucas enjoys a nice evening with Sophie and her friends, who experience sharing their information with an attentive and eager audience.

Lucas, who is securely attached, loved a childhood of feeling established and comforted by way of his parents. By contrast, Dan was raised by loving parents, but they were not always able to comfort his anxieties as a child. Still, he typically felt glad in relationships till his last year of college, while he advanced his first critical dating with Susan. She became highly critical and subsequently cheated on him with his pal; and then she dumped him. Since that time — specifically with girls — he has tended to be self-important, to feel extraordinarily stressed with ladies, and to experience rejection. His way of coping with this was to stay quiet, so he didn't display his inadequacies and could hopefully avoid rejection. This frequently backfired because women felt they couldn't hook up with him.

If, like Dan, you tend to doubt your worth and are judgmental of yourself, studies in self-compassion offer you some good news. There's sturdy evidence that self-compassion is partnered with the ability to look at reality more objectively, have insight, and be inspired to attain personal growth — all of which will let you conquer your tendency to self-verify your attachment-related tension. In aid of this, there's additionally proof that self-compassion permits you to feel a greater social connection, more content, and to have a greater sense of wellbeing (Baer, Lykens, and Peters, 2012; Barnard and Curry, 2011). Importantly, with self-compassion, you experience a greater sense of happiness, love, and affection even after failure, or while dealing with your barriers or weaknesses. So, in a sense, you can't lose. You can put yourself out there, in the face of failure, wrestle with private demons and continue to view yourself undoubtedly as someone who's learning and growing.

The result is a happier you with greater chances for a happier dating experience. (I say more possibilities for happier dating because, regardless of what you do, you still want your partner to work with you to nurture successful courting.) If you discover it hard to be compassionate toward your own struggles, then you need to expand compassionate self-cognizance. Each part of compassionate self-focus provides an essential element to getting unstuck. To review, the foremost factors are self-consciousness and self-compassion.

Awareness of feelings

- Identification of your feelings

- Conscious experience of your feelings, awareness of mind

- Objective attention of mindfulness

- Allowing yourself to see how you perpetuate your attachment-related tension

- Maintaining a serious attitude about yourself while emotionally linked to your reviews

- A reflective stance that lets you consider viable motives for your feelings, thoughts, and behaviors, in addition to the ones of your partner

- Understanding how your way of perceiving yourself and your partner might be biased self-compassion

- Acceptance of your self

- Compassionate response on your misery

People excessive in self-compassion go through times of pain just like everybody else. They need assistance from others; they need connection, help, and advice. However, they have several distinct advantages. They are more accepting of themselves; they may be better at nurturing wholesome relationships; they could make higher use of appropriate advice or comments after they make mistakes or are suffering from unique troubles, and they may be more resilient.

If you do not have a whole lot of self-compassion, you — sadly — cannot just will it into existence. However, through compassionate self-awareness, you could expand it and nurture greater happiness inside yourself and within your dating. If you are not in a relationship, it could still help you to experience yourself, in addition to finding a partner more effectively.

To make it clear how this works, recall Peter. He is a forty-five-year-old bachelor who would love to marry. When he meets Amanda, he's enamored with her and decides to devote himself to this new relationship. He pours himself out to her, hopeful that she will agree and love him. He is

173

capable of being so open because he overrides and tries to ignore his fears that she might reject him.

With time, however, he's aware that he's beginning to sense distance from her (recognition of feelings). He's conscious of being essential to her. He thinks of matters like, "She can really be annoying," or "It's not an awful lot of fun spending time with her" (consciousness of thought). At first, he thinks that perhaps there's simply not enough chemistry. But while she can't get together with him one night, he misses her desperately, fears she'll go away, and is crazy to win her love again (recognition of feelings and thoughts).

At that point, he realizes (with the help of mindfulness) that the problem is not a lack of chemistry between them. He can see that he has instinctively protected himself from harm through being critical of her. With this insight, he can view his feelings as understandable and self-compassionate. So as opposed to ending the connection as he had been considering, he has a brand new option — to withstand his fear of rejection.

After a lot of support and encouragement from friends, he talks to her about this worry, permitting himself to be genuinely open. This ends in them working together on building emotional intimacy — a connection beyond simply sharing the information in their lives. Without the focus of thoughts and emotions, mindfulness, and self-compassion, Peter's story might not have ended so well. He might have concluded that there was really no chemistry and hurt Amanda. Or supposing they had married, he might have vacillated between being essential and remote, on one hand, and passionately engaged in trying to win her over or reassure himself of her love, on the opposite. Alternatively, she might have felt a lack of focus on him and eventually broken off the connection.

If he were still ignorant of his battle while she did this, he could have been feeling pressured, not able to understand what went wrong. And if this became a repeating pattern for him, he might have questioned rejection.

Compassionate self-awareness is effective because it provides a way for humans to work with their inner conflicts, as Peter did. If you're extremely disappointed about a few issues to your relationship, you or your partner demanding you "stop worrying" won't fix anything. It could accentuate your emotions — turning them into a storm so one can weigh down any effective attempt to deal with the issues at hand. At times like this, compassionate self-cognizance can help you to understand your struggles and process them in a concerned, gentle manner — in the end, permitting you to nurture the connection you need.

I can think about no more succinct or more eloquent way to describe compassionate self-cognizance than this statement (broadly attributed to playwright August Wilson): "Confront the dark parts of yourself and work to banish them with illumination and forgiveness. Your willingness to wrestle with your demons will cause your angels to sing. Use the pain as fuel, as a reminder of your strength."

In the following two chapters, I will help you with simply that. Later we offer direction for how to illuminate your internal studies — the dark and the not so dark ones. We offer hints for studying to give yourself a means of forgiveness and compassion. As I've explained, you've got true reasons for keeping your attachment-associated anxiety — it can feel like survival. If you try to reduce this tension, your resistance will run deep. This is authentic even if you consciously want to change and you could be healthier for it. So in case you are set on enhancing your courting or looking for one, treat it with diplomacy. Expect inner resistance and plan to persist. Instead of looking to overpower (or bully) yourself with needs to be changed, try to "make friends" with your reports.

As with any new friends, you may try to recognize and understand them. Also, don't forget, the elements for you which might be holding directly onto attachment-associated tension are trying to protect you, so interact with them sensitively. Begin by opening yourself as much as possible to the idea of change. Then you may move on to becoming more aware of and accepting of your feelings, gaining focus and attitude concerning your thoughts, and increasing your capacity to mentalize. The following sections offer ways to develop in each of those regions. Try the exercises that appear to touch what you need to grow. Do them in whatever order seems to be most useful and repeat exercises as you see fit. Be alert to a firm preference to avoid an exercise or an aversion to thinking about some precise phase. That might be a misguided attempt to using your unconscious to protect you and can display a vital place in which you need to do some work. So provide critical consideration to what that section is addressing and attempt to work on it. Resist the temptation to "push through the ebook" without soaking up what the exercises offer. Feel open to work on any unique exercises for a while, or even to go back to an exercise later on after reading further.

To expand a steady romantic courting, it enables you to be aware o your ambivalence towards opening yourself up to the vulnerability that this purpose perpetually brings. It's this awareness that allows you to view the way your attachment-associated tension prevents you from improving your courting. For instance, Andy knew conversation was essential in relationships, so he compelled himself to speak with his wife about her current distance. However, because he failed to acknowledge just how threatened he felt, he unconsciously included himself by turning the message in an opposed and accusatory manner. "We might as well not be married. Honestly, you're of no use to me!" This served to create more distance. Had he been more aware of his speech, however, he would have avoided getting hurt and hurting his wife. He might have spoken about his fear, which would have been much more likely to elicit a concerned reaction from his wife.

By going through your ambivalence, you are going through your fears that you are unworthy of love (or that your partner may see you this manner) and that you could lose the connection you want so much. This isn't any small task. But by doing it, you'll avoid self-sabotage attempts and improve your love life.

As you gain this cognizance, approach your fears and anxieties gently. Take small steps. Prepare yourself for alternatives with the aid of consciously working along with your ambivalence. Do this in any way that works for you, such as giving yourself time to consider your struggles, journaling, speaking with a supportive buddy, or expressing your struggles creatively, perhaps via painting or writing poetry. It's very essential to recognize that more self-consciousness does not suggest you have to act any differently. So eliminate this stress from yourself.

For instance, acknowledging that you are feeling disrespected by the help of your companion does not suggest you need to leave her. However, when you are stuck in a terrible trial, more cognizances will help you to see how your styles of conduct are painful. This increases the chances that you'll want to do something different. To this end, it would help to speak with someone who can help with your problems or to read a terrific self-help book. In some cases, you would possibly even find help in a unique movie. For instance, watching the film Silver Linings Playbook (2012) might help you discover love and happiness even within your emotional struggles.

Facing ambivalence is something you'll want to do time and again as you task yourself to become more steady and reply in another manner in relationships. Every time you are ready to take the next step, just do it. Be careful to no longer fall into the trap of thinking…and rethinking…and rethinking your state of affairs. Remember the adage, "strike when the iron is hot"? Now's the time to use it. People have difficulty identifying their feelings for many reasons. If you have trouble with this, it may be because you're out of touch with them. Or possibly you don't know the phrases to best describe them. Or you might be focusing more on your thinking. Or glossing over your emotions with trendy descriptions, consisting of "dissatisfied" or "bothered."

If you've got attachment-related tension, you're likely to discover that your emotions frequently build depth and seem to meld collectively, leaving you feeling overwhelmed by using one large, unidentifiable mass of emotion. Simply acknowledging and labeling these feelings can deactivate and calm the amygdala, the part of your mind that triggers your severe distress.

By finishing the following exercise, "Identifying Your Emotions," you may learn how to pick out and differentiate your feelings. In doing so, you'll also reduce their depths and your distress — so that you will, in turn, discover ways to tolerate them better. Then you'll be in a better role to nurture more in-depth dating by communicating them to your partner in a productive way.

By going with this method, it's crucial to develop the potential for each confidence in your feelings and close yourself off to them. For instance, you may help yourself genuinely experience your fear of rejection, so one can feel "right" and you can genuinely enjoy yourself. But then, after a while of connecting with that feeling, you may find which you are just digging yourself deeper into a depressive hole or developing a bigger sense of emotional chaos. I have observed in my clinical experience that people generally have a sense of when they're productively connecting with their feelings versus simply making themselves more dissatisfied. The concept is that, just as with any new skill, you need to live inside the gray zone — a little beyond what is comfortable, however, not so far out that you are overreaching. When experiencing your feelings becomes counterproductive, it's time to move off this manner and engage in something comforting — perhaps lunch with a buddy, watching a film, or playing a walk in the park.

Exercise: Identifying Your Emotions

You can discover clues to your feelings in the present-day situation, your bodily sensations, and your behaviors. So display those on an everyday basis. If you tend to do well with structured help, make a chart with a column for each of these areas, as defined below. Or, if you prefer, think of the regions — it is helpful to do this at prescribed times, including the morning or at meals. You may also communicate about them with a relied on buddy or your partner. Although I mentioned the distinction between thoughts and emotions within the last section, the separation among these things is not absolute.

People's thoughts or perceptions of a state of affairs regularly affect their feelings. For instance, you could feel sad when you mirror your perception of yourself as having no feeling toward others. In this case, it's miles more accurate to say that you are feeling "worthless" or "pathetic" than to label your emotion as "sad." Even though these words reflect thoughts or judgments, they add an emotional experience. Similarly, after finding out that your partner has had an affair, your hurt and anger could mix with your thoughts to leave you feeling betrayed. So you don't forget your emotions, you might discover that they're mingled together with your thoughts.

Exercise:

Date: By recording the date, you can keep track of the types of feelings you have, particularly if you go back to this exercise at different times.

Situation: Observe the state of affairs when you are distressed. For instance, you become aware that your husband isn't home for dinner for the third time this week, and he tells you almost as an afterthought that he'll be late only when you phone him.

Sensations: Pay attention to the way your experience is framed. For instance, whilst you found out that your husband was going to be home late, you felt tight in your chest or even developed a headache quickly afterward. In different situations, you may feel hot, dizzy, or shaky, or you might have "butterflies" in your stomach.

Behaviors: Note what you did in response to the situation. In our example, you would write down that you go off the cell phone quickly and then cried or threw something.

Thoughts: Note your thoughts about the situation, yourself, and your partner. In this column you may write, "It's not okay for him to keep doing this. I'm surprised at what I'm doing incorrectly that's pushing him away. I assume he is probably having an affair."

Emotions: As you tune in to your sensations, behaviors, and thoughts, do unique feelings arise? Rather than trying to force a label onto what you think you "should" be feeling, try letting the names of the emotions bubble up. For instance, you may write, "Frustration, anger, anxiety, the worry of rejection, hurt and betrayal." If this proves too hard, consult the list of emotions on the chart that follows. To be clear, this list includes labels for basic emotions (including joyful, indignant, and afraid); combinations of emotions (surprised + unhappy = disappointed); and combinations of emotions and thoughts (joyful + perceived success = proud). I offer these combinations to will help you understand the various nuances of the emotions that you may feel, so see which ones you connect with. You may need to copy this chart and keep it handy during your day. Remember that you are probably experiencing some of these feelings — even a few that war with each other. By figuring out your emotions, you are acknowledging your experience.

This is fundamental to your, coping with your emotions effectively, and speaking with your companion in a way that permits him to understand you — and hopefully to connect with you, too. So, especially in case you conflict with figuring out your emotions, this exercise is well worth practicing.

List of Emotions

HAPPY • At ease • Ecstatic • Hopeful • Pleased • Thankful • Blissful • Elated • Humorous • Proud • Tranquil • Calm • Energetic • Inspired • Relaxed • Cheerful • Excited • Lighthearted • Relieved • Comfortable • Exhilarated • Optimistic • Satisfied • Wonderful • Content • Glad • Peaceful • Serene • Delighted • Grateful • Playful • Spirited

COMPETENT • Adept • Capable • Independent • Powerful • Self-reliant • Adequate • Composed • Indestructible • Privileged • Strong • Arrogant • Confident • Inspired • Savvy • Thoughtful • Brave • Courageous • Invincible • Secure • Together • Cocky • Important • Invulnerable • Self-confident • Worthy

Tolerating Your Emotions

As you open up to self-cognizance, it's important that you are capable of tolerating your feelings. You need to be able to undergo emotional misery at the same time as resisting the urge to try to make it disappear right now, which might save you from completely connecting with, acknowledging it, and coming to terms with the experience. Neural plasticity — the capability of the mind to change — is what enables this working-through manner to help you ultimately relate in another way to your feelings. You can grow tolerant of your emotions with the help of exposing yourself to them, however carefully, and not so much so that you feel crushed. You can do that through mindfulness and meditation. You also can do it by coming close to your emotions with interest.

Because being curious about your thoughts on the matter and wanting to recognize more about them, such interest will assist you in staying open to your feelings despite a few anxieties. This, in turn, will enable you to explore them more thoroughly and to discover and integrate that means from your newly identified emotions. This advantageous focus permits you to develop a better tolerance for distressing emotions.

One manner to develop interest is by virtually completing the previous exercise, "Identifying Your Emotions" — but choosing to treat it with open and curious thoughts.

Exercise: Befriending Your Emotions

As you develop an ability to tolerate your feelings, you could work on being more open to them — or even befriending them. To befriend your feelings is to invite them into your life because you notice the value in them. No, you wouldn't actively need to experience dissatisfaction; however, you can be glad about the blessings in a particular scenario and the related feelings it conveys in your life. For instance, you may admire your loneliness because it motivates you to meet new people or a special person.

You can start the procedure by considering the unique emotional conditions and think about the following:

- Do your emotions assist you to understand the scenario or your interaction better?

- Are your emotions a warning that there's a problem you need to address?

- Are your feelings and expression of empathy, assisting you to connect with your companion or others?

Through these questions, you could deal with your feelings as you would with a friend — with an open heart. It enables you to recall that emotions are a part of being human, even when they're painful. It also enables you to be an affected person with yourself; studying to befriend your emotions may be a long-term venture and a talent that you'll need to practice for the rest of your life.

As explained in the last chapter, your mind impacts you on many levels. If you pay attention to and grow your consciousness, your attachment-associated anxious thoughts, and their results, you might begin to question them. Sometimes you can replace them with new, healthier questions for the old self-destructive mind. For instance, you might choose to focus on your tendency to repeat, "I haven't had a female friend in so long; I'm this type of loser." You can begin by noticing every time you say this to yourself, and then replace that thought with the better message: "I've had a dry spell for a while, however, I've been in relationships before and I can find a special person again."

If you practice thinking about this new message, you can help yourself start to think it automatically. Don't be hard on yourself if this doesn't work. The approach has its limits. If the brand new statement is in direct struggle with your perceptions, repeating it until it's wholly convincing, simply as you may never convince yourself that night is day, irrespective of how commonly you label the moon as the sun, it may never become convincing.

What's most crucial now is that you end up more aware of your mind and the way it affects you. By doing this you are setting up a solid foundation for the know-how of your feelings and beliefs about yourself and your relationships, and for relating in a different way to those feelings and beliefs. For instance, again recall having the idea, "I haven't had a girlfriend in so long; I'm this sort of loser." You may come to recognize that every time you have that thought, you are giving yourself an injection of depression and hopelessness. Once you comprehend this, you've got a better understanding of the way your emotions work. Making this connection is a critical step in relating more positively to yourself.

Exercise: Changing Your "Thought Bubble"

Your poor thoughts — either within the shape of self-criticisms or in the shape of perceptions that your companion does not value you — perpetuate your attachment-associated tension. To trade these, or at least lessen their impact on you, complete the chart on the next page. As with everything else I've addressed, it's very important to be affected by the person in yourself.

You are working to change a manner of being that has probable been with you since childhood, so it'll take time to establish a new way of wondering and feeling. Spend a while reviewing the chart. Journal it. Talk with a supportive friend. Think about the approaches that have caused issues in yourself and your relationships — and till you are aware of when and why your wondering is currently creating problems for you.

To start, make a chart that you can fill in each day. Label 5 columns: Date, Situation, Attachment-Related Anxious Thoughts (associated with your partner and you), and Effects of Thoughts on Feelings and Behaviors and Disconfirming Evidence.

Date: Noting the date will help you preserve the time of patterns, specifically in case you experience this all through exceptional periods of time.

Situation: Write down details about the scenario related to your current, past, or potential partner that prompted you to end up dissatisfied. For instance, you are probably dissatisfied whilst your boyfriend is going out with his friends.

Exercise: Choose to Be Curious

One of the best methods to bolster your potential is to mentalize to consciously emerge and be more curious about yourself or your partner. In this exercise, you will develop distinctive methods of viewing your partner. More importantly, the aim is to focus on more than one view, not simply to find the "right" one. This will assist you to find a hundred and ten opportunities in preference to right away clamping down on a single one with one judgment, like a metallic trap.

Do this in four steps:

1. Choose a situation. Pick a few behaviors or interactions — nice or poor — to focus on which you have questions about, or that you could be wrong about. Example: Sybil's neighbor Russ invited her out on a date. Because she struggles with low vanity and because he knew she hadn't been out with anyone in some time, she figured it was a "pity date."

2. Check-in with what you feel and wonder. Do an intensive activity of this — you might even want to seek advice from the "Identifying Your Emotions" exercise earlier in this chapter. Example: Sybil might first be aware of feeling insecure, careworn, afraid, and anxious. Then she might realize that, despite herself, she became excited, felt desired, drawn to Russ, and was intrigued by the opportunity of a date. She may also realize that she turned critical of herself — questioning how she became an idiot and feeling indignant that she gave her hopes up.

3. Consider feasible explanations. Once you can connect to and pick out your feelings and thoughts,

don't forget the viable reasons why the incident happened, using what you recognize about yourself and your companion. Example: Sybil assumes that Russ asked her out because he was bored, he pitied her, he wanted to just go out as friends, or — maybe — because he preferred her.

4. Find out the truth. For the functions of this exercise, this last step isn't necessarily very important — that is, what's crucial here isn't that you guess correctly about the motivations of your partner. Instead, the reason for this exercise is to open yourself up to consider opportunities as you continue to relate to how you feel. After you are open, you can discover a solution that is supported with the help of the evidence around you and that resonates with the inner you as accurate, even though it isn't necessarily comfortable.

Example: While Sybil might no longer ask Russ outright why he asked her out — despite certainly wanting to — she may want to look for signs and symptoms of his intentions. For instance, it'd imply one intention if he said that his other friends were all out of town this weekend, however, another if he confessed that he found her attractive and wanted to ask her out for a long time.

<u>Note</u>: The examples in this exercise center on seeking to recognize someone else. But you may also complete this exercise to focus on yourself. As I've noted, we may be blind to our intentions and struggles.

Exercise: Getting to Know Your Partner from the Inside Out

Mindfulness permits you to become emotionally keyed in toward your partner because it can provide you with a window into their world. It does this by supplying you with a more detailed knowledge of their experience. Your aim is to truly see the world through your partner's eyes, along with what they observed, felt, and thought. Keep in mind that you don't need to agree with them. Also, you don't need a grainy home-film view, instead of a high definition, being-in-her-shoes experience. Keep the following in mind when your partner is speaking with you about an experience (it can be something from going fishing to mourning the demise of a parent).

DO:

- Give her all of your attention — no multitasking.

- Tell your companion you're interested in hearing about the topic.

- At suitable times, ask for more information or explanation, so that you can absolutely "get it" — the information and her thoughts and her feelings.

- Note nonverbal cues for a better experience of the depth and satisfaction of her experience.

- Be open to her perspective, especially while it doesn't hurt yours.

- DON'T:

- Multitask — not even to just take a look at that incoming text.

- Interrupt, unless you are burdened and need clarification.

- Assume what she is thinking or feeling.

- Try to remedy a problem (unless you're asked to).

- Tell her she's wrong about the facts or her experience.

With time, your efforts will pay off. You will feel closer to your partner and he or she will be closer to you. This may even go a long way toward soothing any unnecessary fears of rejection.

Final Thoughts on Self-Awareness

Self-consciousness requires patience. It must arise as a top of the line degree of emotion between newly growing attention and old perceptions of yourself and your companion. Otherwise, self-verification will override your new focus, whether it is thought, emotions, or mentalizing. So, remind yourself of this. Think, journal, complete the exercises in this book, speak with your partner, and share with other reliable family and friends. Above all, persist in your explorations of the latest approaches of connecting with your own exploration along with your partner.

CHAPTER 4

Exercise: Heighten Your Attraction with Activity

Sexual attraction is vital in keeping your romance alive, whether you're with a prospective companion or in a longtime courting. And this enchantment is intensified by bodily arousal. Research has proven that physical arousal may be generated with the aid of any source, from exercise to experiencing excessive emotions, which includes anger, sadness, and excitement (Pines, 2005). But your mood also influences appeal: you're more likely to experience attraction to someone and to express this when you are in a great mood in place of an horrific one. If attachment-associated tension has generally driven your appeal, then it's crucial to discover different, healthier approaches to excite sexual enchantment and stimulate romantic interest. Here are some exercises to do alone before your date or with your partner — though you may need to think about your ideas.

- Bicycling

- Hiking

- Rollerblading

- Playing tennis

- Brisk walks

- Dancing

- Going to concerts

- Watching emotionally charged movies — say action, comedy, or romance

- Traveling to new locations

Engaging in these physically arousing and laughing experiences can open up a whole new world for you. Rather than counting on your worry of rejection to stir up your passion, you may feel attracted to a person who additionally lets you feel emotionally safe.

Exercise: Show Your Love

One of the best methods to show your love is to show it with physical affection. You can do this in limitless approaches. You might hold hands, hug, offer a shoulder or foot massage, or maybe lightly touch your companion again. And, of course, there's making love. Equally crucial to touching your companion is simply enjoying whilst your partner touches you. A sure way to experience love is to melt and soak up that touch. If you're distracted by thinking about different things or reduce the contact through wondering if it doesn't suggest anything, then you are, in that moment, failing to soak up your partner's love. So pay attention. Touch comes more easily to some human beings than others. If you and your partner tend not to be physically affectionate, then you may want to work on touching more — and maybe even get your partner to join you.

Many humans make it a part of their routine to hug every morning or evening (I'm speaking about an extended taking-each other-in hug, not a quick clench-and-release). You and your partner might attempt that or attempt giving each other foot massages. You may also start by cuddling at the same time as watching TV. With practice, you'll find that the soreness lessens and is replaced by a sense of comfort and warmth.

Exercise: Make Compliments a Habit

Just as physical contact can support your courting, so can words. They can be expressed in powerfully touching approaches. For instance, there was the fantastic moment in the movie As Good as It Gets (1997) when obsessive-compulsive, misanthropic, and generally offsetting Melvin (Jack Nicholson) says to Carol (Helen Hunt), "You make me want to be a better man." Your compliments don't usually have to be that dramatic.

Often, the great compliments are easy observations of appreciation of your partner. You could tell your companion that he's a superb cook or that she is a great mother. Then there is always the heartfelt, "I love you." When you share the best sentiments on an ordinary basis, you each can't help feel better for it. So, if your dating is brief on compliments, change that. Make it a habit to praise your partner at least once a day. And in case your partner is also quick on compliments, communicate with her about this. You could even ask her to study this section, then make a pact for each of you to complement each other one time each day for a week.

Check-in at the top of that week to see how it went. Let each other know how being complimented felt. That's an excellent thing to do after you receive a compliment. Then you can recommit to every other week. Keep doing this — making a dedication to praise each other every day for a specified length of time checking in afterward. Repeating this exercise will help turn it into a habit that you actively encourage together.

Exercise: Loving Actions

Doing satisfactory things for each other comes naturally in the beginning of dating. He buys you flowers. You send him a considerate text. You both recognize and celebrate special occasions, which include birthdays or huge accomplishments. Often, however, relationships go through periods when companions take each other without any consideration and don't try to worry. During those times, companions experience disconnection and feel alone or even rejected. If you're in a new relationship and your partner isn't always displaying concern (or may be very inconsistent in doing so), then you could be smart to question whether or not he is the proper partner for you. Ask yourself whether the strength you experience is special strain or worry of rejection and whether or not your partner's attachment style is triggering this. It's critical that you and your partner make efforts to do things that say you care and want to make each other happy. However, you may not really understand what would, or does, make your partner happy, and the same may be true for him. This possibility is uncomfortable for many humans. They think that their partner must realize what makes them satisfied without being told and that telling their partner what they prefer invalidates the motion itself. However, it's unfair to expect others — even those who love you — to read your mind.

Also, to be upset because of that is to miss the factor that when your partner wants to pay attention to what makes you happy and act on it, it says something important about him. Explicitly stating what you need is a no-lose proposition. With this in mind, examine the next exercise on soliciting for what you want. If you feel ready to address it, ask your partner to read it, too, or explain it to him. If either of you is hesitant in doing this, make an effort to think and talk about what makes you hesitant.

For instance, some human beings feel that sharing what they want makes them as vulnerable as much as being rejected, or might make them seem needy. Hopefully, with the help of speaking openly, you may reassure each other that you simply want to make each other satisfied. After you've talked, you might feel geared up to working on the exercise as it is written; or you might choose to simplify it, as I will explain in the first step.

Make a list of moves your companion should take that would make you feel loved. This could be something that he already does or used to do or something which you'd like him to do. Be concrete. For instance, you may write: deliver me water for my nightstand each evening, hold my hand when we walk together, tell me you like me, sit next to me whilst we watch TV, or accompany me to a basketball game. Steer clear of inquiring about something that has been a source of conflicts or tension. Also, do not proportion this list yet. If you want to start a piece more slowly, you may pick out just two moves that you would love the other to do. Pick ones which you think might be acceptable — maybe something that you're partner used to do or has done on occasion.

Later, after you have gotten good results, you could move to doing this exercise in its complete form. Talk about what it might be like to share your lists. Share each important and negative feeling. You might begin by saying that you are looking forward to hearing his requests. But you may also share that you are uncomfortable with the exercise. Perhaps you're concerned about sounding worrying or having him reject everything you ask for. As you talk, your partner should listen and offer help. Then reverse roles. (If this essentially repeats a conversation you had while preparing to do this exercising, that's okay. Reinforcing help for each other is frequently useful.)

Read your lists to each other. One companion reads every item slowly so the other companion has a chance to hear, and don't forget the request. The two of you may want to talk about some items, perhaps reminiscing about what your partner used to do or clarifying what is being asked. Remember that these are requests, not demands. At the end, the listening partner ought to name one or more items that he's comfortable with and consents to do.

In the unlikely event that the listener isn't comfortable with any items, both of you may gain from him explaining his discomfort, reaffirming a desire to make you happy, and suggesting different loving moves. Take time to speak through this exchange until you are both comfortable. Then trade roles; the listener turns into the one who shares and vice versa. Review the exercise after about one week. Share thoughts and feelings about the exercise. In particular, express appreciation for each other's efforts. You might need to repeat the exercise, perhaps making improvements based on feedback, or maybe add a few more ways you particularly love.

On Being Grateful

If you and your companion enjoy each other's company, it seems natural that you would experience and develop gratitude for having your partner in your life. Unfortunately, your potential to be thankful in this way might be impaired with the aid of attachment struggles. Instead of feeling correct about your companion's expressions of affection, you might see this as a trait belonging to him along with him being a loving person in place of relating to something about you. So, in place of feeling better about yourself, you are probably thankful to your partner for loving a person as unworthy or fallacious as you. To complicate matters, you may build resentments in the direction of your partner, who will necessarily fail at times to meet your needs. Or, even whilst you do experience your perfect dating, you might discover that it is a painful reminder of relationships in your past that started happily and soured over time.

In these different approaches, your superb feelings can transform into sadness and strengthen a sense that you are unworthy of affection. If you relate to this experience, you must learn to soak up your companion's tremendous view of you and to preserve in mind ways in which you value your partner. Review the next two exercises, which are designed to help you do that. Complete whichever one you think would possibly work for you or do both if you wish.

Exercise: Mindful Gratitude

You can grow your gratitude by deciding to be aware of and appreciate the qualities in yourself and your companion. Consider doing one or more of the following practices on an everyday basis: focus on what your accomplice values in you; work on experiencing popularity and gratitude for those features; truly listen to her expressions of affection and permit them to wash over you as you soak them up; focus on what you respect, admire, and are drawn to on your partner. Just think about these matters.

As positive feelings arise, acknowledge them and choose to be grateful for your companion. When you are disenchanted with your companion for any reason, go back to these thoughts as a matter of balance to (but not to dismiss) your negative feelings. This is vital to do if you tend to lose sight of your partner's positive traits while you are upset with her. Focus on the ways that you and your companion are an outstanding team. Reminisce about good times you've had — whether they were earlier in the day or years before. Accept, absorb, and treasure all the ways that the two of you create a loving relationship together. Keep in your thoughts that those practices are likely to show full-size and lasting results if you make them a regular part of your life.

Exercise: Carry Gratitude

The following exercise for nurturing gratitude is primarily based on research conducted by Brine, Gasco, Petty, and Horcajo (2013). These studies found that people can get rid of thoughts, just like they do waste — by throwing them in the garbage. Similarly, they can keep and treasure thoughts, similar to trinkets; and in doing so, be laid low with them. This exercise is structured so that it will help you nurture gratitude in a similar way for effective characteristics on your partner and your dating. Write about the characteristics you appreciate from your partner. Study it over slowly, permitting yourself to clearly feel desirable about your partner and be glad about having him in your life. Write down the characteristics of your courting that you appreciate. When you complete this, examine it slowly, permitting yourself to really feel good about your relationship and to be pleased about having it in your life.

Keep the list close by and accessible. Research indicates you are much more likely to be influenced by this paper if you keep it with you such as in your pocket. Whether you keep it there or elsewhere, you may gain an advantage from reading it regularly. This will help you to naturally keep these thoughts in your mind and your attitude. Just as with dancing, relationships need work and practice. While you must depend upon your partner, you should also feel balanced inside yourself. Acknowledge there could be mistakes, however, focus on the best qualities. Completing the steps in this chapter will allow you to move in harmony with your internal self and with your partner.

Live a Happier, Healthier Life: How Your Partnership Can Heal You

Imagine that the plumbing in your house has a slow leak, and you haven't checked your month-to-month water bill in thirty years. Now you observe it and you're stunned! It's no longer simply that you allowed the leak to hold on for a long time; the quantity of water you wasted through the years is enormous. Now suppose it was possible to measure the strain on your body. Imagine that your strain machine hasn't been checked since infancy to see how much energy you have expended adapting to life's diverse stresses. Bear in mind that some of the strength lost to strain is not renewable. That is, it has seeped away over time because of pressure, and just like the water from that leaky pipe, can't be retrieved. The "invoice" you receive for your total strain costs is what Bruce McEwen (2000) and different scientists call static loads. It's referred to as the rate we pay for the strain required of us during life. All static loads involve four principal physiological systems: cardiovascular, autoimmune, inflammatory, and metabolic.

Over time, if we accumulate a heavy static load, we can expand infection in all or any of these four systems, including heart disease, diabetes, arthritis, and fibromyalgia. Our relationships with others, and especially our primary devoted relationship, strongly affect our all static load, by both reducing and increasing it. Yes, it may work both ways, and how it works for you is largely up to you. Some individuals — islands, for example, also many waves — choose to forego relationships, at the least number ones, in preference of solitude because they find committed relationships too stressful. Others chose to pursue relationships, or find themselves feeling abused, neglected, or otherwise dispirited by way of the realities of their marriage or union.

The stress they come upon in their relationship places them at risk for infection. Others still find themselves in relationships that help them to thrive, energize, and destress. This chapter focuses on the health hazards as well as the fitness benefits that include a number one relationship. As you read it, recollect what you might do to make sure that your courting mitigates strain and always contributes more to your fitness and happiness. If you ask a pair to identify the main sources of stress in their lives, they probably won't point to their relationship. In many cases, that answer is exactly as it should be. However, for some couples, this represents a blind spot. Although they may be alert to strain in other areas in their lives, which includes stress caused by a boss at work or economic problems, they're in denial when it comes to stress in their relationship.

Be Annoying but Never Threatening

I regularly tell couples that within their couple bubble they can do or say things that can be annoying, however, they can never be threatening in the eyes of their partner. You can be annoying with a grin to your face, and laugh about it later. But threats undercut your security. Moreover, it doesn't count what you keep in mind as threatening; if your conduct is perceived as threatening by your partner, you then have a problem.

That said, right here are some behaviors that usually are considered threatening:

- Raging

- Hitting or other kinds of violence

- Threats against the connection

- Threats against the individual

- Threats against others important in your partner

- Holding on for too long and not letting move

- Refusing to restore or make proper a wrong

- Withdrawing for periods longer than an hour or two

- Being continuously unapologetic

- Behaving habitually in an unfair or unjust manner

- Putting self-serving pursuits ahead of the connection an excessive amount of the time

- Expressing contempt (devaluation; e.g., "you're a moron")

- Expressing disgust (loathing or repulsion; e.g., "you are making me sick")

Lynn Katz and Ahmed Gottman (1993) studied the deleterious results of partners' expressions of contempt and determined that not only does this behavior put the connection in danger, but it has a disruptive effect on their children's behavior. Gottman (2004) ranks contempt, which he defines as that which includes disgust, disrespect, condescension, and sarcasm as the primary predictor of divorce. If any of the behaviors indexed apply to your courting, then you put your relationship in danger and the destructiveness on your partnership remaining safe and secure.

Remember, partners are wired together: wherein one goes, so does the other. If you're threatening or if your partner feels threatened, etc., it can't be comfortable for you either. You owe it for your relationship to do away with all threatening conduct. If this means looking for the help of a therapist, as within the case of Ralph and Lorraine, I can't think about a better investment you can make in your courting.

Exercise: Seeing the Blind Spots

Do you think you could have a blind spot in terms of the extent of stress at home? If you answer yes to the following, pressure may be hurting your courting.

1. Do you or others in your circle of relatives have frequent and unexplained physical ailments, along with digestive problems, insomnia, continual pain, continual fatigue, or allergies? Any autoimmune or inflammatory problems?

2. Are you or others in your circle of relatives struggling from depression or anxiety or emotional overload?

3. Do you or your companion say or do things that might be perceived as threatening?

4. Do you and your partner fight frequently?

I understand these may be hard questions to ask, but if you don't ask, you risk losing not only your best courting but also your health and wellbeing.

Healing within the Couple Bubble

It's no longer sufficient to minimize stress at home: your courting can and needs to function its best for fitness and health. Consider how every other couple treated this issue.

Tenth Guiding Principle

The tenth precept is that companions can minimize each other's stress and optimize each other's fitness. I found this fit for the last section of this book as it ties up with what we have already discussed. Bottom line, through adhering to the principles presented in the preceding chapters — for example, a pair bubble based totally on actual mutuality, well-skilled ambassadors that preserve your primitives in check, an up-to-date owner's manual on your courting — you avoid causing strain to yourself and your partner. In so doing, you actively foster physical and emotional fitness and well-being for both of you.

Here are a few helping ideas to guide you:

1. Manage each other's strain. In past decades, techniques for stress reduction have ended up ever more popular. You might already be familiar with these — time management, eating regular meals, getting sufficient sleep, exercising, relaxation, to name a few. However, what's lacking in most techniques to stress control is the important thing partners can play. I'm suggesting that, as specialists on one another, who understand how your brain functions, you could add the size of stress reduction on your owner's manual. Knowing the three or four things that make your partner's experience bad gives you a bonus in terms of detecting strain and even waiting for it. You and your partner can help one another in lowering stress by making sure you

interact in healthy sports and obtain balance in your lifestyle.

If you observe your companion isn't getting enough sleep, step in, and help find a solution. You may volunteer to tackle more household chores until he or she has stacked up on needed rest. If your partner is slacking in his or her exercise routine, this might be the time to visit the health club. Or if your partner had a hard day at work, perhaps tonight is the proper evening to lease that comedy you've talked about watching.

2. Be aware of the unique experience of stress. As you help control your partner's pressure, bear in mind that everyone experiences strain differently. For example, a tax audit that causes you to lose sleep might be visible as a minor blip on the radar of your partner's screen. In this case, you each bring a distinctive history and set of emotions to monetary matters. So be careful not to impose your assessment of strain on your partner. Remember, you're a professional on him or her. So whilst you assist your partner to lessen pressure, you do so on his or her terms. And, of course, your partner will reciprocate in kind.

3. All illness is induced through strain, but stress can irritate any illness and make it worse. As when you and your partner age, you will come upon the natural challenges

all our bodies face as the years advance. Know, however, that via loving each other fully, studying the way to defuse struggle and make choices which might be pro-relationship as opposed to pro self, and wiring yourselves for love, you stand the best chance of living a cheerful, healthy, and pleasurable union.

CHAPTER 5

All intimate relationships contain some miscommunication, disagreement, or struggle. However, if you tend to focus with tunnel vision on how you can save yourself from being rejected and earn your partner's love or attention, you'll probably use your strength to avoid such troubles. You probably tend to brush your own needs and emotions underneath the rug. This is your way of defending yourself. In time though, you'll ride over the ever-growing bump in that rug as you emerge aware of how you experience your relationship. You'll understand the hurt that has accrued and even sense irritation with your partner.

This is a sample that can't make you happy. Fortunately, there's a better way. Through compassionate self-focus, you can discover how to value yourself, tolerate your feelings, and be willing to chance vulnerability. You will even be more open to compliments from caring humans in your life. As a result, you may be more capable of the venture of sharing along with your partner, and be able to really listen to your partner's experiences without being sidetracked by how they affect you.

The result of drawing closer relationships in this manner is that you'll be emotionally taken, and successful at nurturing an intimate connection. If you are still essentially open, caring, and expressive when struggles arise, then you are in an ideal position to keep your connection as you figure out how to resolve or manipulate the problem. This section will guide you through the system of coping with conflict in just such a positive manner.

Asking for Support

The technique of directly requesting what you want gives you and your partner the chance to work together on nurturing your relationship.

You may discover it useful to focus on two primary practices:

1. Share your feelings, wants, and wishes.

2. Ask without delay for what you need from your partner.

Examples:

Heather is disappointed when her boyfriend Art is going out with his friends. She stews in her feelings, however, she does not share them with Art — which makes her experience more distance from him and makes her worry about losing him. Finally, she decides to tell him, "When you go out with your friends, I experience abandonment and feel I'm no longer essential to you. I need you to have fun with the guys; however, that is without a doubt tough on me." They discuss the problem and he explains that he enjoys spending time with his buddies, but this isn't a replacement for her. After a few discussions, they agree that he will usually provide her enough notice about his plans so she can make plans, too. He agrees that on nights when she finally ends up home on her own, he will call or text her while he's out or on his way home — so she'll realize that he's taking her into account.

Sally regularly goes on business trips, leaving Max to feel lonely and to question if she cares for him. He has always been supportive of her career, but he struggles with her touring a lot. He loves spending time with her. He explains this, being certain to express that he wishes her to pursue her dreams. Though they don't come to any answers for their differing needs, they do feel they are supportive of each other. They reaffirm their dedication to the relationship and agree to speak by text day by day while she's away.

Of course, not all conditions come to operate so well. When your conversations become poor, make sure to go back to them at a time when you are calm. Your goal is to find a manner to feel cared about and to join with each other on an emotional level, even when you are addressing a hard problem. The next exercise assists you to clear up some of these thorny troubles.

Exercise: Starting a Difficult Conversation

Your tone of voice can set the mood when talking to your partner. The Gottman Institute, which conducts studies related to marriage and relationships, expected the final results of a fifteen-minute communication within the first three minutes. They could also predict which couples would divorce and which would stay married (Gottman and Silver, 1999; Carrere and Gottman, 1999).

So carefully undertake how you start a communication and follow these hints:

- pick an emotionally impartial time to speak.

- Timing isn't quite the entirety, however, it's a lot. A tough verbal exchange can only go well if each companion is in a top enough emotional and mental state to deal rationally and flippantly with it.

- State the trouble succinctly. Don't rely on what your partner has done, or what the state of affairs is, the real problem is how it affects you. So state the problem succinctly and get on to the actual difficulty — how you are laid low with it. Do not blame. Going on about all of the horrific things your accomplice has done or pointing to faults in his character will make him defensive. You won't feel better and he will be more emotionally remote.

- Focus on your part in it. As much as you would like to lash out or run from your accomplice when he's disillusioned you, you'll want him to recognize and care about you. The simplest manner he can do that is if you balance your thoughts and emotions.

One technique of doing this constructively is to use "I" statements. When you start a sentence with "I," you're telling your partner something about what's going on for you — opening your world to him. By contrast, while you start a statement with "you," you are probably being critical of your partner and final conversation. For instance, when saying, "You never do anything romantic anymore." This gets your point across, but you're much more likely to get the response you're looking for by saying, "I wish you'd do something romantic, like when you used to bring me flowers for no reason." Or if you and your partner discussed his tendency to drop his grimy clothes on the ground and he agreed not do it anymore but then he did. You might say, "I'm annoyed with you for doing that. It makes me feel unloved and that you think I'm your maid. I feel so alone." Compare that with saying, "You are a slob and completely insensitive. I don't know why I try to speak to you about anything." Need I say more?

Of course, you may also use "I" statements to be critical, such as, "I think you are an idiot." And "you" statements may be sensitive, such as, "You have tried to be supportive, but every so often I'm so disappointed that I can't take it in." So, after I work with patients, I have them try pointing out how they make the announcements; this generally suits the individual that they are talking about. The point is that you need to open up about yourself, giving your partner the chance to truly "get," support, reassure and understand you.

Be honest about your feelings. You may want to spend some time getting in touch with and figuring out your emotions. If you're unable to do this, try the "Identifying

Your Emotions" exercise in chapter 3. Once you're honest about your emotions, share them with your companion. For instance, you may say, "I feel sad," or "I'm lonely." State what your partner can do to satisfy your desires. Be specific. This frequently follows from sharing your feelings. For instance, you could say, "I feel unloved, and I need to understand that you truly love me. So you could hold my hand while we're out together or make plans for us to spend time together." Or you may say, "I am lonely and need us to be closer. So I'd like us to spend more time just sitting and chatting over dinner." If you aren't sure what your companion can do that will help you feel better, discuss it together to discover a solution.

Talking Through Conflicts

In addition to sharing your emotions and desires, healthy verbal exchange requires you to concentrate and "get" your partner — not just intellectually understand her, but see situations through your partner's eyes and empathize with her. To do this, you should be capable of expressing your perspective. No cutting off your companion as you give an explanation aimed toward making her accept your truth. No minimizing or denying your partner's feelings if you want to protect yourself from the harm those feelings elicit.

However, as you do this, you do not need to agree with your partner or give up on what you want. It's simply that you and your partner need to take turns listening. You both must be open to sharing, "getting" each other, and speaking together supportively and constructively.

With this approach, you can have a sense of protection even within the most private and vulnerable conversations. As you should be cautious about how you begin a tough discussion, the power of this sort of conversation isn't always what you communicate about, it's about how you do it. For instance, it helps to be aware that you each have biases and are each fallible. Your willingness to look at and admit this could help you be open to feedback, experiences of compassion, readiness to apologize, and potential to forgive. Overall, for a constructive outcome, you have to approach your companion with the rationale to honestly understand him or her, share your experiences, and grow to be emotionally closer. Otherwise, you and your partner will find yourselves living parallel lives, or at odds, as you each try to protect your own perspective.

Here are a few recommendations for communicating effectively. Be a secure haven. I cannot emphasize enough that companions need to feel secure with each other. This can be most effective if nurtured in a conversation with the help of focusing on one partner at a time. If you're addressing a problem, ask your partner to pay attention and try to understand what you're saying. Tell him that you want to make sure you've had a chance to get out what's in your mind, and then make sure he understands it before you shift to his thoughts. (This dovetails well with the previous exercise, "Starting a Difficult Conversation".

If your companion is citing a problem, attempt to understand his attitude. Your purpose is to empathize, to try to get as clear a feel of what your partner is experiencing as you can. This will help you feel for your partner. Also, if your partner feels that you understand and care, he could be less defensive. A top-notch way to show your partner that you "get" him is to reflect what he says. That is, when he's done speaking, mirror back in your own words what he's saying, without delay, about his thoughts and emotions. If you aren't certain that you understand, say so and ask for clarification. Truly listen without interrupting. It's often tougher than it seems since it's natural to get stuck in your reactions. But recognize your partner's misery first. Then, after he feels truly heard, reassured, and valued, you can impart your experience — and he'll be more likely to truly listen. Offer positives.

It's beneficial to make note of things you appreciate about your partner when discussing a hard topic. This can save you from getting flooded by distressing feelings and negative thoughts about him. Instead, you'll be at the least fairly grounded by your emotions in the direction of your partner. It can even send him the message that you appreciate him, even though you are unhappy with a particular conduct or state of affairs.

All of this helps to keep the discussion in greater positivity. Stay on topic. When arguments get heated, it's easy to jump from one subject to another. This may be because you're dropping the floor and you don't want your companion to win. Or it could be because one negative idea results in another, and before you know it you're off on a list of issues that your partner cannot respond to coherently. But, no issues are ever resolved whilst the problem is constantly shifting. Be respectful. Mutual respect is fundamental to intimate relationships, and there's no reason to be rude or insulting to your partner. This is true even when you are indignant with each other. If you have got a problem with becoming overwhelmed and exploding in anger, take it easy. This can consume you personally and erode your relationships. Try applying the language of compassionate self-attention to this problem, locating self-help materials partnered with anger management, or go in search of therapy.

The Gift of Forgiveness

Any two individuals who share their lives and hearts will at some point harm each other. It is probably out of anger, ignorance, or their very own struggles that they can't see past. It may be because of a false impression or — now and again — through caring more about your own happiness than your partner's misery. Feeling harm is painful for everyone. But it could be particularly difficult for someone who struggles with attachment-related anxiety. In those cases, it frequently runs deep, mixing with an experience of being mistaken or unworthy of love. Troubling thoughts, emotions, and recollections can flood the person. And the ensuing self-complaint or hostility toward her or his partner may be effective and destructive.

If you relate to this, then you need to shift past the harm and gain knowledge on how to forgive. By nurturing forgiveness, you may be giving a gift to yourself. It will permit you to pass by anger and bitterness. This is burning in your heart and soul. You also can take it into account as a gift to your partner and your relationship. If you trust that your companion normally has your best interests at heart, regrets the damage he did you, and will now not repeat the offending behavior, forgiveness will permit your relationship to heal. If you do not consider any of that, then it might be time to move on. In that case, forgiveness may be your way of wishing your partner no harm.

Forgiveness doesn't suggest pronouncing that an offending behavior is acceptable; rather, that you'll go past it. Even so, you could change your behavior towards your partner because of it. For instance, if your partner is an alcoholic, you may require that he get treatment and refuse to keep alcohol in the house. However, if he gets suitable help and does his best to stay sober, you might forgive him by no longer keeping his past against him in the present. This is not something you can just determine in a moment; it includes a process of coping with emotions within yourself and in your relationship. At a later time (after you've forgiven him), if he has relapsed, you may still air these concerns, but you'll accomplish that in a manner that focuses on the present. It wouldn't make sense to talk about this in the terms of the past, however, the forgiveness method requires that you don't simply dredge up the past without a current reason to do so.

Jack Cornfield, a noted trainer of meditation, says: "Forgiveness is a vow now not to carry bitterness into the future…to determine to surrender desire for a higher past" (2011). Again, nurturing forgiveness takes time. So have compassion in your struggle and be patient as you head toward healing.

Exercises:

Learning to Forgive: What follows is a sequence of exercises that can help you to move toward forgiveness. Appreciate being forgiven. Happiness researcher Sonja Lyubomirsky (2008) shows that humans start in the direction of forgiving by appreciating a time when they had been forgiven. You might recollect a time you have been forgiven through a parent, pal, or former partner. Think about why they might have forgiven you and how it felt to be forgiven. Consider the way it helped them, you, and your relationship. Apply understanding and compassion. Keep in mind what upsetting behaviors you have been unable to forgive as you read the following: Complete the "Identifying Your Emotions" and "Befriending Your Emotions" exercises in Chapter 3. You can also return to the "Mindfulness" section in chapter 3. Keep the hurtful incident in mind as you do. Read it through and complete the exercises "Choose to Be Curious" and "Getting to Know Your Partner from the Inside Out." This should help you to admire the state of affairs and your partner's actions from a more informed perspective. To be able to forgive, you'll want to exercise having compassion for yourself and your companion. As you undergo this process, the aim is to be able to maintain your own comfort while additionally empathizing together with your partner.

This can be tough to do, however, it's vital. To help with it, practice going back and forth between the exercises that connect you with your own enjoyment and those that assist you to empathize together with your partner. Create a feeling of safety. For you to forgive, you must be feeling emotionally secure. So you want to take reasonable measures to help you feel secure in the present. For instance, in case you still need to end your marriage after your partner has had an affair, you'll want to know that she is devoted to your relationship and is no longer in touch with the other man. Or if your companion has put you in the debt, you may also want to have control of the money until he receives assistance and earns back your trust in this area.

Remember that through forgiveness, you aren't forgetting what occurred. You are clearly relegating it to the past. As you can see in the above samples, you can learn from what happened and make decisions based on them. But when you forgive, the distinction is that you focus directly on the pain, not try to make him "pay" for what he did, and instead focus on caring and send compassion in the direction of your partner. You will have times when you feel pulled to experience past harm and anger. You will need to talk yourself out of using them. When the thought of the offending behavior comes to mind, respond with self-compassion. For instance, you may remember, "Of direction, those are hard reminiscences to leave behind." Then remind yourself that the state of affairs has been addressed, or is being addressed now. If you can, flip your thoughts to this gift.

You might find it useful to ask your companion for support. You must try this in a no blaming manner. For instance, you might say, "I'm definitely feeling insecure now. I'm afraid you're going to have another affair and I'll feel like a jerk for ever trusting you again. I need some reassurance from you now." (The previous exercise on how to start and speak through tough conversations helps you with this). Finally, with reassurance you are more emotionally secure, concentrate on the positives in your courting and on the affection he expresses to you. Depending on your unique situation, you may want more guidance and help in this area. If so, search out self-help materials or couples remedies.

CONCLUSION

Closing Thoughts

Through studying and applying the facts in this ebook, you've got a new appreciation for your difficulties in romantic relationships. You can see that they are expressions of struggles with the way you relate to yourself, in addition to your partner. You can also perceive the path toward a satisfied, healthy romantic relationship, and make large strides down that path. Part of the beauty of being in a secure relationship with a companion is that it additionally encourages and reinforces a stable feeling in you. If you do the work laid out on this e-book, you will become happier — on your romantic courting, for your different relationships, within yourself, and in your life. There's no doubt that this takes focus, persistence, and effort. But the advantages are tremendous!

Seeking Professional Help

By completing this e-book, you've taken fantastic strides, but it nonetheless might not be sufficient. For instance, if your partner is not doing her part despite seeming to need to be together, or you appear to be unable to break free from your patterns of anxious attachment, then seriously consider couples therapy. Or in case your attachment-related anxiety overwhelms your efforts to have an experience of self-concern or you're potential to feel safe in relationships, bear in mind your remedy. You can take insights from this book to therapy, and you may even help your remedy along by way of sharing them in sessions so that the therapist can integrate them into the treatment method.

Ahmed Bowlby (1989), the person who first proposed the idea of an attachment machine, explained that remedy can help humans increase more stable sorts of relating to others (Mikulincer and Shaver, 2007). It is critical as a way to have a feeling of your therapist as a secure haven and a secure base. With this foundation, you will be supported in pursuing private activities and opportunities for growth, and you'll also feel safe to explore your insecurities.

Your therapist can guide you in gaining more focus on painful feelings, terrible self-perceptions, and difficult behaviors. You'll discover ways to consciously understand your personal well-intentioned, however inaccurate, efforts to develop an experience of safety and reassurance in your relationships. Although you truly need to find an experienced and successful therapist, it's essential that you also discover a professional with whom you have an awesome rapport. Because therapy involves heartfelt discussions, one can leave you feeling vulnerable, so you need to feel as emotionally safe as possible with your therapist.

In many ways, the work you do in therapy naturally develops your ability for compassionate self-awareness. Moreover, with the help of compassionate self-awareness, you may communicate more directly about it. This discussion can facilitate the work of healing, helping you to efficaciously change your self-perception and your ways of relating to others.

You Can Do This

Your dating issues can feel overwhelming, however, when they do, keep in mind that there's a course to happier, healthier connections. You can find a life partner who's there to support, encourage, and love you, just as you can be there to help, encourage, and love him. The manner to do that is what this book has been all about. It gives you a way to think compassionately about your experiences at the moment, permitting you to nurture yourself and your relationship (or your relationship skills). Together, these moves will free your love from insecurity.

When I see companions in a well-maintained couple bubble, one outstanding characteristic is their capability to calm, influence, and manage each other, like the way expert dads and moms do with their children. Both partners appear to have read and punctiliously studied the owner's guide for their relationship and each other. Each is accustomed to operational details that nobody outside of the bubble is going to recognize. As an example, these partners recognize what pushes the other's buttons. When the other is feeling awful, they know why. And they know how best to remedy matters. They know the proper words to say, or deeds to perform, they can elevate, relieve, excite, soothe, or heal one another.

Are such people in ownership of a perfect partner chromosome? Trust me, no. Do they have some sort of mystery superpower that permits them to manage their partner emotionally? Well, maybe. As I said before, a number of us were given a better start in life than others, with lots of great interactions with safe adults who were interested in and curious about us. We all come to the table with primitives that don't want us to be harmed, and ambassadors that at times may be annoying. Truth is, we may be, all of us, pains in the rear. And yet, in my exercise and research that is exactly what I see couples in stable relationships doing. It is a conscious choice they make. They agree to take each other on "as is," and take responsibility for each other's care. As specialists who understand their partner, they do what's essential to relieve the other's misery or to increase his or her happiness. To many partners who discover themselves at the mercy of each other's moods, this kind of understanding may appear to be a mystery superpower they'd do almost anything to obtain. The position of primary partner is a huge one: it entails taking accurate care of another human pain in the rear. Both partners need to grow to be professionals on one another. You can consider it as a type of pay-to-play version of romance, and it is - make no mistake, a payment on your future.

ANXIETY SERIES

"Certain of the interest shown on the topic, thanking my public for the daily follow up, I list those that are the current projects published, hoping to do something nice!"

Good reading...

ANXIETY in RELATIONSHIP expanded edition – Rewire Your Brain From Attachment Theory Of Anxious People. How To Break Bad Habits, Toxic Thoughts, Crucial Conversations, Worry And Return To Talk To Anyone

COUPLES THERAPY WORKBOOK – How to Reconnect With Your Partner Through Honest Communication. Overcome The Anxiety In Relationship And Build A Strong Emotional Intimacy Laying The Foundations For Unconditional Love

ANXIOUS in LOVE - How Stopping the Spiral of Toxic Thoughts and Anxiety in Relationship Overcoming Conflicts and Insecure of Couple. Abandonment and Separation is Never a Relief!

JEALOUSY in RELATIONSHIP – Manage Your Emotions By Overcoming The Fear Of An Insecure In Love. How To Sweep Away Anxiety With New Communication Skills, For A Healthy Couple

*"For better enjoyment, you CAN find all this titles also in audio format, on **Audible**."*

MY FREE STEP-BY-STEP HELP

I'll send you a free eBook! Yes, you got it right. I'll send you my future projects, in preview, with nothing in return, just leave a realistic review on this eBook, believe me, it will be very helpful to other readers.

Thanks in advance!

Leave me your best email and my staff will send you a copy as soon as possible:

theresamillerauthor@gmail.com

Don't go yet; One last thing to do…

*If you enjoyed this book or found it useful, I'd be very grateful if you'd post a short review on **Amazon**. Your support really does make a difference and I read all the reviews personally so I can get your feedback and make this book even better.*

Thanks again for your support!

Made in United States
North Haven, CT
25 February 2023